STRATHCLYDE UNIVERSITY LIBRARY

30125 00291373 8

£145 80

ML

KU-214-124

ANDERSONIAN LIBRARY
★
WITHDRAWN
FROM
LIBRARY
STOCK
★
UNIVERSITY OF STRATHCLYDE

This bo

Man and
Accidents Offshore

13667786

Man and Accidents Offshore

An examination of the costs of stress among workers on oil and gas rigs

VALERIE J. SUTHERLAND, B.Sc., M.Sc.

CARY L. COOPER, B.S., M.B.A., M.Sc., Ph.D., F.B.Ps.S.
Professor of Organisational Psychology, UMIST

LLOYD'S LIST
DIETSMANN (INTERNATIONAL) NV

UNIVERSITY OF
STRATHCLYDE LIBRARIES

Lloyd's of London Press Ltd.
Sheepen Place,
Colchester, Essex CO3 3LP

U.S.A. AND CANADA
Lloyd's of London Press Inc.
817 Broadway
New York, NY 10003 USA

GERMANY
Lloyd's of London Press
P O Box 11 23 47, Deichstrasse 41
2000 Hamburg 11, West Germany

SOUTH EAST ASIA
Lloyd's of London Press (Far East) Ltd.,
903 Chung Nam Building
1 Lockhart Road, Wanchai
Hong Kong

© Valerie J. Sutherland and Cary L. Cooper
1986

British Library Cataloguing in Publication Data
Sutherland, Valerie J.
   Man and accidents offshore : an
   examination of the costs and stress
   among workers on oil and gas rigs.
   1. Offshore oil industry — North Sea —
   Employees 2. Offshore gas industry —
   North Sea — Employees 3. Job stress —
   North Sea
   I. Title II. Cooper, Cary L.
   622'.338   HD8039.0342N6

ISBN 1—85044—082—4

All rights reserved. No part of this publication may be reproduced, stored
in a retrieval system, or transmitted, in any form or by any means,
electronic, mechanical, photocopying, recording or otherwise, without the
prior permission of Lloyd's of London Press Ltd.

Text set in 10pt on 12pt Andover
by Communitype, Wigston, Leicester
Printed in Great Britain by
The Eastern Press Ltd., London and Reading

D
622 · 338
SUT

Preface

This study aimed to investigate psychosocial and occupational stress among personnel employed on oil and gas exploration and production installations in the Dutch and United Kingdom controlled sectors of the North Sea. An assessment was also made of mental well-being and job satisfaction, with a focus on the incidence of accidents offshore. Utilising interview and questionnaire method, quantitative data, from 194 respondents located on thirty-one installations and engaged in a variety of occupations, were analysed. Factor analysis identified seven underlying thematic variables which were entitled, "relationships at work and at home"; "site management problems"; "factors intrinsic to the job"; "the uncertainty element of the work environment"; "living in the environment"; "safety", and the "interface between job and family", and accounted for 49.7% of the variance. With the exception of the Dutch production platform personnel, it was found that this occupational group were much less satisfied with their jobs than their onshore counterparts, and although overall mental well-being compared favourably to the general population, levels of anxiety were significantly higher. Concern is expressed for an unacceptably high proportion of individuals offshore scoring within the psycho-neurotic out-patient norm category for sub scales of obsessionality and phobic anxiety. Using multivariate analysis, it was found that "relationships at work and at home" was a strong predictor of both job dissatisfaction and mental ill-health. Type A coronary prone behaviour was also a significant predictor of reduced mental well-being and increased accident rates offshore. Job dissatisfaction and reduced mental well-being may result in poor performance, poor productivity, reduced physical health and an increased vulnerability to accidents. Emphasis on the importance of "relationships" suggests that attention should be paid to improved team working, group development and improved on-site management. The findings may also have implications for improved offshore safety in terms of selection of individuals most suited to offshore employment. However, further research is needed to establish whether the environment is eliciting and reinforcing

deleterious behaviours or if a particular type of individual is attracted to
this way of life.

March 1986   V.J.S.
                                                                      C.L.C.

Contents

List of tables

List of figures

1 Introduction

Diebold (1964) states, "the effects of the technical revolution we are now living through will be deeper than any social change we have experienced before". From this technical revolution have emerged the "new" industries with all the elements of the unknown and uncertainty that they bring.

Not the least of these is the oil and gas extraction industry. It might at first seem a paradox to call this industry new when one considers that the first oil well was dug in Southern Iran in about 500 BC (Cooper, J. 1984). Even though the first offshore oil well is recorded as early as 1896 off the coast of California, the majority of offshore drilling activity has taken place only in the last 30–35 years.

Although many companies working in this offshore "arena" may claim 60–70 years of operating experience, it is without any doubt that each new discovery area brings its own unique set of problems. The current North Sea exploration and production projects are no exception to this. The deep water environment and the extreme and difficult weather conditions have proven to be a great technological challenge for the industry, demanding new strategies and equipment in order to exploit these "blue" and "black gold" resources. This development of the industry will continue; the recent award of the 9th Round of offshore leases (May, 1985) includes the most challenging areas yet, the Rockall and Faroes Troughs, and the Central North Sea, which appears to have a number of significant gas/condensate reservoirs, will be both technically difficult and expensive to develop. This means that every day, thousands of offshore workers are exposed to new and challenging work environments. Yet we know very little about the effects of this environment on these people working and living on offshore drilling rigs and production platforms.

Life in our complex, industrial society, characterised by uncertainty and rapid change, is an acknowledged source of stress (Toffler, 1970). For some individuals this provides a challenge and a form of gratification (McLean, 1979). Indeed, no-one can live without experiencing some degree of stress all the time (Selye, 1956). In this respect stress is not bad,

1

but is the spice of life; it is essential to growth, development and change, and thus performance. But some individuals in some organisations are exposed to increasingly stressful conditions to the extent that physical and psychological health is impaired. This results in the individual not realising his full potential, to the cost of industry and himself; that is, lost time due to illness or accident, forced early retirement or premature death. We simply do not know how this new offshore working environment affects the people involved in the short term, nor the long term. Questions arise such as, "Is there a burn-out factor?" "Will there be changes in decision patterns in time?" (Hellesøy, 1985).

It is true that certain occupations are seen as stressful because the content is perceived as being hazardous, and this perhaps is the general lay-person's view of the working conditions on drilling rigs and production platforms. In reality, although there is a hazardous content, it is hazardous to the layman but not necessarily to the competent, trained employee. It may be that the offshore worker is aware of the danger and makes his own value judgement by accepting or rejecting it.

But, without empirical evidence, hearsay exists with all its inherent and concomitant misperception, rumour and exaggeration. Such hearsay is a poor foundation on which to build a venture which is successful in both financial and humanistic terms. Therefore, it is important that we understand the phenomena of work stress; and so we must be able to define, identify, measure and ultimately optimise stress levels to enable each individual to realise both his organisational and personal goals. Stress need not be destructive in its consequences, but can be managed. Stress that may lead to "distress" should therefore be minimised, prevented or eliminated.

Although interest in the topic of occupational stress continues to grow, there are still vast gaps in our knowledge and understanding. The extent and significance of the problem throughout industry is not well documented. This study therefore attempts to contribute information, insight, explanation and ultimately prescription in two main ways: Firstly, to add to the existing, but minimal knowledge and understanding of occupational stress among blue-collar workers; secondly, to investigate into an industry that is virtually unexplored in terms of quantitative, empirical data. Thus the major objective of this project is to identify the primary sources of psychosocial and occupational stresses which contribute to stress related illness and/or may be a contributing factor to the incidence of accidents among those employed offshore in the North Sea oil and gas industry.

2 Rationale

Our understanding of the nature of stress at work increases as data from research into many different occupations begin to take on a definite pattern. Research findings generally support the idea that the sources of stress of a particular occupation, together with certain personality characteristics, may be predictive of stress manifestation in the form of mental ill health, coronary heart disease, frequent and severe accidents at work, job dissatisfaction, excessive alcoholic intake, and marital disharmony etc. (Cooper, 1985); and that one symptom may exacerbate another. Cooper (1981) thus proposes the following model (Figure 2.1), indicating six major sources of occupational stress interacting with the individual to result in both organisational and individual symptoms.

The manifestation of individual symptoms as a response to work stress will be discussed in more detail in Section Four, "What is Stress", and the sources of stress proposed in Professor Cooper's model (Figure 2.1) will be reviewed in Section Five, "Stress: A Research Model". However, in this section a rationale for the present study of stress among offshore workers in the oil and gas extraction industries will be proposed in terms of the negative effects of stress at work for society, the organisation and the individual. The "literature review", Section Three, indicates only minimal enquiry into this unique offshore working environment of the North Sea; and most of this is of a descriptive and anecdotal nature. But perhaps it is a sign that many of the initial operational "headaches" are finally overcome, in that attention is now beginning to focus more firmly on the people employed offshore. It may be that organisations are slowly understanding the importance of recognising "people" as their most important resource (Flamholtz, 1971; Cooper, 1984; Womack, 1985), and that counting the cost of human resources has tremendous potential benefit in both humanistic and financial terms.

Awareness of some of the very high costs of stress related illness to industry is gradually having an impact. The American Heart Association estimate the economic costs for individuals with cardiovascular disease in the United States were U.S. $46 billion for 1981. Mismanaged stress is one of the causes of this disease. Stress manifestation in the form of

3

Figure 2.1 Stress—A Research Model

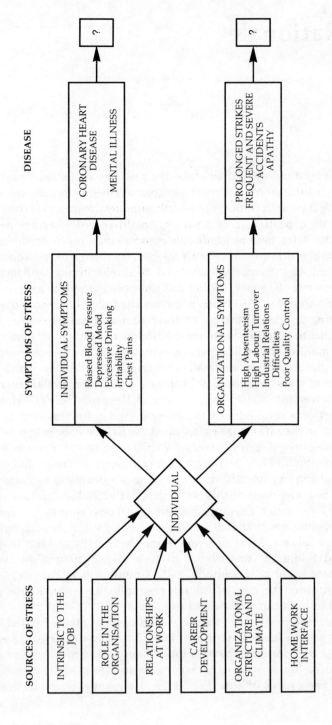

Source: Cooper (1981)

alcohol abuse has been estimated to cost U.S. $40 billion annually (Quick & Quick, 1984). Ivancevich & Matteson (1980) estimate that the total cost of distress may be in excess of 10% of the U.S. gross national budget.

Stress or distress at work results in absenteeism, and stress related illness in the form of diseases of the circulatory system is listed as the second largest "cause" in the table of reasons for sickness and/or invalidity benefit in Great Britain 1975/1976 (Office of Health Economics, 1979). Figure 2.2 shows the number of days in thousands of certified incapacity for the period 7 June 1976 to 6 June 1977. Circulatory disorders constitute for 15% of the total days lost. However, it must also be remembered that these figures do not include short term absence of 3 days or less and that not everyone is included in the National Insurance Scheme.

The first report produced by the National Association of Mental Health, *Stress at Work*, 1971, suggested that 36.5 million days were lost in a year through poor mental health and stress related symptoms. More recent figures indicate that this is now in excess of 40 million days (Tinning & Spry, 1981) and costs more than industrial injury (Taylor, 1974) and strikes (Gillespie, 1974).

The following information (Table 2.1) shows the extent to which various countries have been successful in combating death due to coronary heart disease, that is, an increase or decrease in mortality rates due to ischaemic heart disease. It is perhaps illuminating to note that Norway is included in the "decrease" section, whereas the U.K. and Netherlands are in the "no change", and this no doubt reflects the serious attitude taken by the Scandinavian countries towards controlling the effects of occupational stress. Also, to date, the Norwegian controlled sector of the North Sea is the only area to receive attention from researchers attempting to identify and quantify sources of psychosocial stress among offshore workers on drilling rigs and production platforms (Hellesøy, 1985). This research will be discussed further in the next section, the literature review.

In total, diseases such as myocardial infarction, ischaemic heart disease, diseases of the circulatory system, including pulmonary circulation and other heart diseases, were responsible for the deaths of more than 22,000 males in the 15–54 age group in England, Wales and Scotland in 1982 (W.H.O., 1982) and figures for the Netherlands are reported at 4,084. Although death from these diseases in the U.S.A. in 1980 claimed the staggering number of 80,000+ males in the 15–54 age group, coronary heart disease rate is finally falling there for the first time this century. But, in England and Wales an increase of 6% in male deaths was reported from 1970–1979 and Scotland now heads the world league table

Figure 2.2 Sickness and/or invalidity benefit: days of certified incapacity in the period 7 June 1976 to 6 June 1977, by cause, Great Britain, thousands

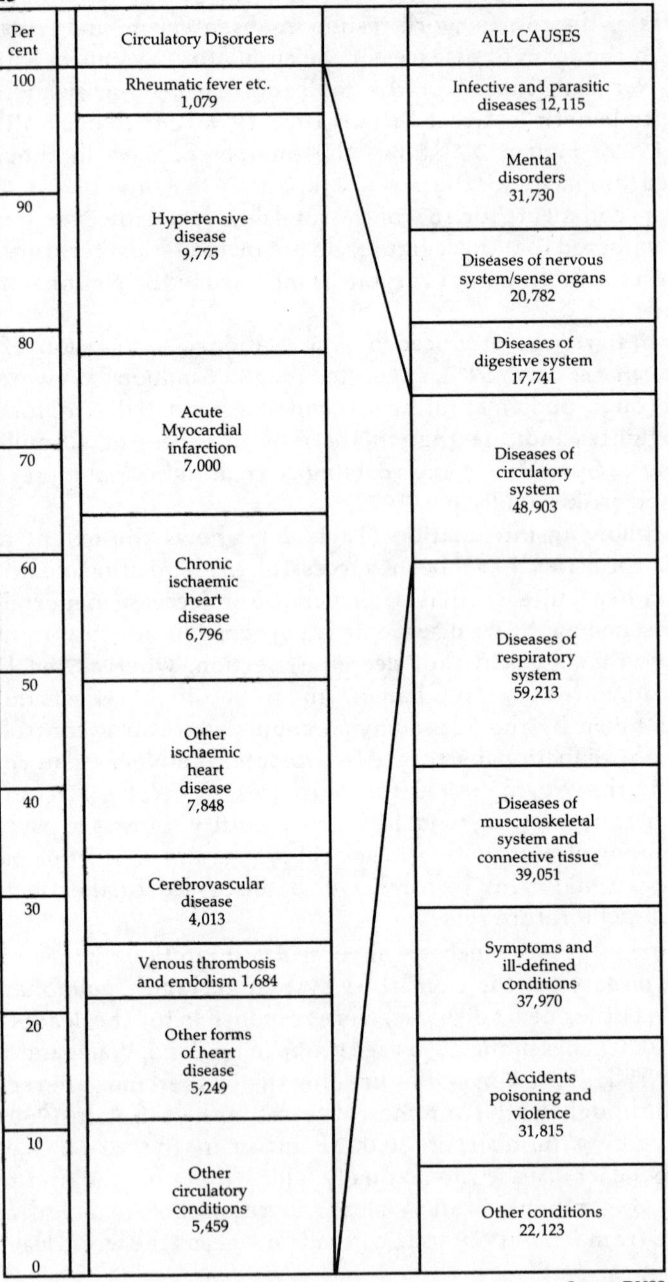

Per cent	Circulatory Disorders	ALL CAUSES
100	Rheumatic fever etc. 1,079	Infective and parasitic diseases 12,115
90	Hypertensive disease 9,775	Mental disorders 31,730
		Diseases of nervous system/sense organs 20,782
80		Diseases of digestive system 17,741
70	Acute Myocardial infarction 7,000	Diseases of circulatory system 48,903
60	Chronic ischaemic heart disease 6,796	
50	Other ischaemic heart disease 7,848	Diseases of respiratory system 59,213
40		Diseases of musculoskeletal system and connective tissue 39,051
30	Cerebrovascular disease 4,013	Symptoms and ill-defined conditions 37,970
	Venous thrombosis and embolism 1,684	
20	Other forms of heart disease 5,249	Accidents poisoning and violence 31,815
10	Other circulatory conditions 5,459	Other conditions 22,123
0		

Source: DHSS

Table 2.1 Groups of countries listed according to the trends of the annual change (%) of mortality from ischaemic heart disease for the 40–69 male age groups in 1968–1977

DECREASE			NO CHANGE	INCREASE		
5%	3–4.9%	1–2.9%	0%	1–2.9%	3–4.9%	5%
	U.S.A.	Australia	Austria	Denmark	Romania	Bulgaria
		Belgium	Czechoslovakia	France		Poland
		Canada	Fed. Republic Of	Ireland		Yugoslavia
		Finland	Germany	Hungary		
		Israel	Netherlands	Sweden		
		Japan	Italy	UK & N. Ireland		
		New Zealand	Switzerland			
		Norway	UK—England &			
			Wales			
			UK—Scotland			

Source: *World Health Organisation Quarterly Report* Volume 35, No. 1 — 1982, p. 19.

of deaths caused by heart disease. Overall, death due to cardiovascular disease heads the table of causes of deaths in England and Wales in 1976 (Table 2.2).

Table 2.2 Top 20 causes of death in 1976; males death rate per million population, England and Wales

		Rate
1	Acute myocardial infarction	2,678
2	Cerebrovascular disease	1,200
3	Cancer of trachea, bronchus and lung	1,110
4	Myocardial degeneration	1,051
5	Pneumonia	994
6	Bronchitis	717
7	Cancer of stomach	289
8	Cancer of prostrate	192
9	Cancer of large intestine (except rectum)	186
10	Motor vehicle traffic accidents	171
11	Aortic aneurysm (non-syphilitic)	152
12	Hypertensive disease	142
13	Cancer of rectum	139
14	Arteriosclerosis	138
15	Cancer of bladder	123
16	Cancer of pancreas	119
17	Influenza	106
18	Suicide	97
19	Chronic rheumatic heart disease	87
20	Diabetes mellitus	86
	All causes	12,527

Source: *OPCS Mortality Statistics DH2*
The leading causes of death were responsible for 78% of the total mortality, the top five alone accounted for 56 per cent. Male deaths from myocardial infarction have increased by 80% in the last 25 years.

In addition to improved dietary habits and the change in attitude towards taking regular exercise as a self-help measure, organisations have begun to recognise the economic costs involved in not protecting their workers from the potentially harmful effects of stress at the workplace (Cooper, 1983). These include the costs of lost time, lost opportunities and compensation claims, where employees have been awarded damages for "cumulative trauma or stress" in instances where the employer has done nothing to minimise the pressures of the workplace.

Contrary to popular belief, coronary heart disease and other stress related illnesses strike at all occupational levels; indeed, the unskilled blue collar worker suffers the highest frequency of deaths from these causes (Table 2.3) and the highest morbidity levels recorded (Table 2.4). It is likely that reaction to stress and manifestation of illness differs between occupation groups. White collar workers may reflect the pressures of work in mental illness and blue collar workers react with physical symptoms and illness (Cherry, 1978; Cooper, 1981; Caplan, 1975). But research into sources of occupational stress among blue collar workers is minimal and many questions still need to be answered. This is further justification for focus on this unique working environment of the offshore drilling and production operations of the North Sea.

In a "new industry", such as oil and gas extraction, it is not known what the short or long term effects of offshore working might be. It is therefore necessary to identify sources of potential stressors in the environment in order to optimise, or minimise them. However, the attitude of organisations in the U.K. and Europe in the main has been that, "stress is none of our business" (Cooper, 1983); it is still looked upon as mollycoddling the employees. Organisations are failing to see that health care or stress prevention at work is financially beneficial, and programmes can be introduced as part of a cost reduction plan when one considers such factors as absenteeism, poor performance, forced early retirement, premature death and costs associated with recruitment and training etc., irrespective of the humanistic or moral arguments. However, it is also necessary to consider "distress" at work as a contributory factor in offshore accidents, and the relationship between vulnerability and accidents should be investigated. "A person under stress is an accident about to happen" (Warshaw, 1979, p. 193). Two classic studies (Hirschfeld & Behan, 1963; 1966) indicate that stress is a significant contributor to the occurrence of industrial accidents, and that it is also related to slow recovery process and prolonged disability. Whitlock *et al.*, (1977) shows that work related stressful events may immediately precede automobile and domestic accidents as well as industrial accidents. The lifestyle and working environment offshore is acknowledged as dangerous, arduous and socially isolating. Living and working offshore present the physical hazards one would expect in a densely populated construction site or factory with additional specific dangers (Elliott, 1985). For example, from exposure to certain chemicals or toxic gas and the ever constant noise, which may vary from mildly irritating to

Table 2.3 Deaths by major causes and types of occupations, 1970–1972 (standardised mortality rates = 100)

Causes of Deaths, Persons Aged 15–64 (Males)	Professional and similar	Intermediate	Skilled nonmanual	Skilled manual	Partly skilled	Unskilled
Trachea, bronchus, and lung cancer	53	68	84	118	123	143
Prostate cancer	91	89	99	115	106	115
Ischaemic heart disease	88	91	114	107	108	111
Other forms of heart disease	69	75	94	100	121	157
Cerebrovascular disease	80	86	98	106	111	136
Pneumonia	41	53	78	92	115	195
Bronchitis, emphysema, and asthma	36	51	82	113	128	188
Accidents other than motor vehicle	58	64	53	97	128	225
All causes	77	81	99	106	114	137

Source: *U.K. Office of Population Censuses and Surveys.*

Table 2.4 Acute sickness and consultations with general medical practitioners, 1974–1975

	Average number of restricted activity days per person per year (males)			Average number of consultations per person per year (males)		
	15–44	45–64	All ages	15–44	45–64	All ages
Professional	9	16	12	2.1	2.7	2.7
Employers and managers	11	13	14	1.8	2.4	2.7
Intermediate and junior nonmanual	10	21	15	2.0	4.3	3.1
Skilled manual and own account nonprofessional	15	24	17	2.8	4.0	3.2
Semiskilled manual and personal service	16	23	18	2.7	4.5	3.7
Unskilled, manual	21	28	20	3.5	4.8	3.6
All persons	13	21	16	2.4	3.8	3.1

Source: *General Household Survey, 1974 and 1975* (by U.K. Government).

permanently damaging (Ross, 1978; Sunde, 1985). All of these factors are in addition to working in some of the most severe climatic conditions encountered in oil and gas extraction operations.

It is not known to what extent the offshore worker perceives his environment as hazardous and thus a potential source of stress, or whether training to cope with conditions and emergency situations reduces the perception of the environment as physically dangerous (Kasl, 1973). Figures quoted from the worldwide offshore accident databank illustrate this point: The mean annual number of active mobile offshore units worldwide between January 1980 and January 1984 was 560. During this period, accidents accounted for 18 mobile platforms totally lost, 33 units severely damaged, 69 units significantly damaged and 83 minor accidents.

Bohemier (1985), speaking at "Mar-Tech 1985" in Montreal, said, "When one does an analysis of the causes of workplace accidents, it is clear that approximately 90% of all accidents arise from some degree of human error or negligence". Human reliability is a significant factor in developing a "total safety concept" for offshore operations and is a man management function (Forum & Patterson, 1983). It is however difficult to measure or control human behaviours and response, and really impossible to legislate control over motivation to learn, or encouragement of personal responsibility. Human error may be mitigated by attention to issues of selection of personnel, education and training, adequate supervision and communication, attention to personnel problems and creating a raised level of awareness for each individual at risk.

At this point it may be useful to include some definitions. "Hazard" is used to mean a particular circumstance which can cause harm; "Risk" to mean the likelihood or probability of that hazard occurring and "Danger" to indicate the combination of "Hazard" and "Risk" which can be expressed as a mathematical product (Berman, 1981, cited Chissick & Derricott, p. 28). An "accident" is defined as, "an unexpected, unplanned event, in a sequence of events, that occurs through a combination of causes; it results in physical harm (injury or disease) to an individual; damage to property, product, equipment, buildings, etc.; a near miss; business interruption; or any combination of these effects" (Bamber, 1981).

Following are details of offshore accidents and fatalities, for both drilling and production platform workers in the U.K. (Table 2.5) and Dutch (Table 2.6) sectors of the North Sea from 1980–1984. Note, these figures are not comparable, due to the variation in methods of reporting and classification by the different controlling bodies.

Table 2.5 Deaths, serious accidents, and dangerous occurrences by activity — U.K. Sector: North Sea for five year period 1980–1984

ACTIVITY	DEATHS						SERIOUS INJURY						DANGEROUS OCCURENCES						ALL INCI-DENTS
	80	81	82	83	84	5 year total	80	81	82	83	84	5 year total	80	81	82	83	84	5 year total	5 year total
Drilling	-	3	3	3	1	10	15	24	13	10	6	68	25	23	40	25	19	132	210
Production	-	-	-	3	-	3	3	2	1	3	1	10	11	14	15	21	10	71	84
Maintenance	-	1	1	-	7	9	13	22	11	8	10	64	21	26	31	34	27	139	212
Crane Operations	1	-	-	1	-	2	4	1	3	6	6	20	32	29	50	32	62	205	227
Structures*	-	-	3	-	-	3	-	-	-	-	2	2	-	-	7	7	11	25	39
Year Total	1	4	7	7	8	-	35	49	28	29	25	-	89	92	143	119	129	-	763
Five year total						27						164						576	1526

*Incidents resulting from failure of part of the structure of an installation, or from damage due to weather conditions.

Source: Department of Energy, *Development of the Oil and Gas Resources of the United Kingdom* (London H.M.S.O., 1985).

Table 2.6 Deaths and injuries by activity — Dutch Sector, North Sea for four year period, 1980–1983

ACTIVITY	DEATHS					INJURIES*					GRAND TOTAL INCIDENTS
	1980	1981	1982	1983	4 year total	1980	1981	1982	1983	4 year total	4 year total
Drilling	-	-	-	-	0	84	73	126	109	392	392
Production	-	-	1	-	1	22	22	30	49	123	124
Four year total	-	-	-	-	1	-	-	-	-	515	516

(*Injuries/Accidents which result in loss of time of two days or less are not included in these statistics.)

Source: Van de Inspecteur General de mijnen — Rijswijk, Netherlands.

Causal agents of accidents include falls, slips, being hit by falling objects, being crushed, and as a result of the faulty handling of objects and manual lifting. Some accidents are caused by defective equipment or inadequate guarding, but others may be due to ignorance, horseplay or sheer bravura. Lives are still lost because safety equipment and protective clothing are not worn at the appropriate time. Accidents may also be the result of fire, explosion, steam blow-out or exposure to toxic/ dangerous chemicals, and are potentially very serious in these consequences. The International Labour Office (1983) provides a breakdown of common accident injuries: Bruising or crushing 40%; sprains/strains 18%; followed by cuts, abrasions, fractures, back pain and amputation. Gentile *et al.* (1983) suggests that the reporting of "dangerous occurrences", in addition to accidents, would also be helpful in improving offshore safety, in that they might have similar causes to those associated with accidents, and therefore be due in more or less the same proportions to human error.

Inadequately trained personnel are an obvious accident risk factor. An inexperienced worker may not be alert to the potential hazards; lacking awareness of the consequences, carelessness or inattention are frequently stated causes on accident reports. The Royal Society for the Prevention of Accidents states, "the main struggle is not so much against the unguarded machine as the unguarded mind" (cited Chissick & Derricott, 1981). But inexperience and lack of training are not the sole cause of accidents as there are many incidences of accidents among workers with 10 years plus offshore experience. Disruption in working relationships is therefore a factor that should not be overlooked. The attitude survey, undertaken by the Petroleum Industry Training Board (P.I.T.B.) (Livy & Vant, 1979), of "stayers" and "leavers" reveals "teamwork" as the quality rated highest necessary for the job of roustabout and roughneck; and an accepted important safety factor involves effective team working. High levels of stress or distress, and an inability to adjust to the demands of this working environment may result in the jeopardy of the essential "co-operation" element of personal safety on offshore drilling rigs and production platforms.

Toffler (1980) describes the modern cities of today as "Sleepless Gorgons"; and this would be a most apt description when one considers drilling and production installations in the North Sea. Standard offshore practice requires the individual to work for 7 or 14 days without a break, usually for a minimum 12 hour shift each day. Some patterns involve 21 and 28 days working, although Government legislation in Holland has now reduced the 28 days on/28 days off pattern to a 14 days on/14 days off maximum. These shorter "tours" are not so popular with the individuals who may travel long distances to and from the job because it reduces the actual time spent at home.

The International Labour Office (1978) reported that no statistics were available to compare accident rates during different work rotations, i.e. 7 days on, 7 days off versus 14 days on, 14 days off etc. However, limited records suggest that there is a tendency for the accident rate to increase slightly at the start and the end of a "tour", regardless whether it is 7:7 or a 21:21 days rotation. Perhaps, at the beginning of a "tour" the individual has not yet got back into the "routine" or there is disruption of his circadian/biological rhythm as a result of night shift working. Similarly, at the end of a tour, an accident may be due to inattentiveness or carelessness as a result of fatigue, unstable working relationships or because the individual is occupied by thoughts of going home.

Shift work patterns are also variable. A 14 day tour may consist of a mixture of day and night working; perhaps starting the first week on days and then the second week on nights, with a "short-shift" pattern in the middle to facilitate the changeover. Some production platform work involves only day-time working; but overtime working is common in excess of the normal 12 hour day and for some individuals there may be night-time call-outs for emergency repair work. The opportunity to be alone or escape from one's 90 to 150+ fellow workers is rare (and major installations house 300–500 personnel). Sleeping accommodation arrangements vary greatly, but sharing a small two or four berth cabin is common practice. Thus, this "constant company" factor may enhance the potential for interpersonal and/or group conflict. The stress that relationships can cause is perhaps adequately expressed by Sartre (1947), "hell is other people". Comments on accident reports such as, "there should be better communication between workers" and, "to pay more attention to ..." are examples of possible breakdown in team working. This arduous work pattern, combined with disruption in working relationships, severe environmental conditions and isolation from family and friends can have a drastic effect on morale, and ultimately safety consciousness. Productivity may therefore suffer and accidents occur. Accidents must thus be seen as both a symptom and a consequence of stress. A great deal of attention is paid to safety and safety training by all the companies involved in offshore working. Legislation varies within the different sectors of the North Sea (refer to Forum & Patterson, 1983 for a detailed account). Given the annual increase in numbers of personnel working offshore, the number of fatal and serious accidents has shown a tendency to stabilise. This is due in part to improved design, safer operational equipment and systems, but also to the training given to ensure safe working at all times (Noroil, January 1985) and, as time goes by, lessons are learned from incidents as they occur.

In Holland a basic five day safety course is compulsory for all offshore workers, ideally before the first tour of duty, but certainly within two or three work tours. Each worker is required by law to carry a "Personal Safety Logbook" issued by the Netherland Oil & Gas Exploration and Production Association (N.O.G.E.P.A.). It is a form of identification and remains the property of the individual; it includes a record of employers, safety training courses attended, medical examinations, vaccinations, and certificates and diplomas held by the individual. In the U.K., the Health and Safety at Work Act 1974 was extended to include offshore installations as of 26 July 1977. Although no legislation exists for minimum requirements for safety training, all oil companies/operator companies stipulate various requirements for their own personnel, and for contractor personnel working offshore. Courses include fire fighting, inflatable life raft training, Whittaker capsule training (evacuation) and some basic first aid.

Training recommendations are made, for example, by the Working Party of the Health and Safety Commission's Oil Industry Advisory Committee (O.I.A.C.); these included, for 1984, the development of standards for the training of radio-telephone operators, helicopter landing officers and standards for survival.

The Department of Energy produce an emergencies handbook describing the action to be taken in the event of a major emergency, e.g. a blow-out, fire or structural failure. It is the D.O.E. that enforces health and safety in the U.K. offshore sector. Recent legislation (May 1984) applied existing legal requirements for fire fighting equipment, life saving apparatus, emergency procedures and operational safety, health and welfare to gas storage installations and accommodation installations. Presently a proposal is underway for new offshore first aid regulations.

But, as Lord Robens (cited Chissick & Derricott, 1981) states, "the probability of ensuring health and safety of people at their place of employment cannot be solved by legislation and enforcement alone ...., the final solution is efficient management and worker participation". There is therefore a need to ensure that the individuals at risk are aware of the potential hazards and how they might minimise those dangers.

Safety is considered more productive in the long run when balanced against the cost of treatment of injuries, compensation, lost production time, and the replacement of disabled workers. As Reddin (1985) states, "the impact of one accident can have a considerable effect on a company's profit and loss statement". It is reasonable to accept that the economic costs of accidents and accident prevention should be calculated, but this remains a controversial issue. Can meaningful costs be calculated when one considers the question, "What price can be put on a person's life?". Examples of figures, in strictly monetary terms do exist: Hanna (1970) suggests a cost of £220 million in Great Britain, and in the Report of the Committee under the Chairmanship of Lord Robens (1970–1972) estimates ranged from £200–900 million (ILO, 1983). The difficulty in agreeing figures is based on the problem of the hidden variables involved. Heinrich (1959) (cited ILO, 1983) suggests that hidden costs include:

(1) cost of lost time of injured employee;
(2) cost of time lost by other employees who stop work out of curiosity, sympathy or, to help etc.;
(3) cost of time lost by foreman, supervisors etc.:
    (a)   to assist the injured,
    (b)   to investigate the cause of the accident,
    (c)   to arrange for production to be continued by some other employee,
    (d)   and selection, training or breaking-in of a new employee,
    (e)   preparation of accident reports or attend to hearings etc.;
(4) cost of time spent on the case by a first aid attendant/nurse etc.;
(5) cost due to damage to machine tools and/or other property, or spoilage of material;
(6) incidental cost due to interference with production, failure to fulfil orders etc;
(7) cost to employer under employee welfare and benefit system;
(8) cost to employer of continuing wages of the injured employee;
(9) cost due to loss of profit on the injured employee's productivity, and on idle machines;
(10) cost that occurs in consequence of the excitement or weakened morale due to the accident;
(11) overhead cost per injured employee which continues while the injured employee is a non-producer.

In Britain alone, occupational accidents and disease were calculated at an estimated cost of £2,150 million per year for 1978. Estimated losses from alcoholism and vandalism within the industry brought this figure in excess of £3,000 million. This amount, according to Lord Kearton, former president of the Royal Society for the Prevention of Accidents (cited Chissick & Derricott, 1981), was equal to the national income from North Sea oil in 1978. No evidence exists to suggest that these figures could have gone down in the past few years, and there is a generally high level of concern regarding accidents offshore. There is therefore a serious need to take positive steps to improve the situation.

The effects of occupational stress may also be manifested in high labour turnover rates. Livy & Vant (1979) reporting on a major category of offshore worker, the roustabout and the roughneck (the unskilled and semi-skilled manual level workers, see glossary appendix) indicate that, taking an annual figure, company turnover at its lowest level was running at 150% ... and in some cases 400%. Labour turnover correlated highly with age (see Figure 2:3), peaking at 22 years of age; and with length of service (see Figure 2:4). New employees are therefore at risk, irrespective of their age; this is termed the "induction crisis".

Figure 2.3 Typical labour turnover schedule in relation to age

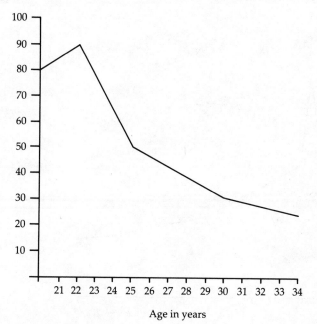

Age in years

The importance of finding the "right" people through selection procedures is emphasised by studies of this nature although, to be really meaningful, the interpretation of such high turnover figures should also include, and take account of:

(a) Whether the individual quit the job or was "run-off" as unsuitable, plus reasons given. Also whether he subsequently found other offshore work where he was acceptable.

(b) Whether the individual quit working as an offshore worker or simply to go and work for another offshore company doing a similar job.

(c)   Whether the individual was "stood-off"; for example, at the end of a particular contract. It is common practice in contracting companies that the same "pool" of individuals move from company to company, as contracts are won and lost, for maintenance work etc. on drilling and production installations. Theoretically then, a worker can stay on the same installation for many years, but work for several different companies. Workers are "taken-on" when needed, and "stood-off" when the job is complete. Thus, turnover rates reported as an annual figure are meaningless.

Figure 2.4 Typical labour turnover schedule in relation to length of service

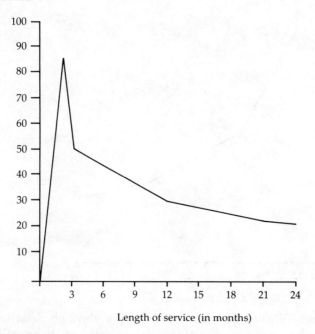

Length of service (in months)

However, "true" high labour turnover figures are deleterious in two major ways. First, it is an important consideration in relation to the high costs of training, especially as courses may be compulsory either before the individual goes offshore or must take place within the first two or three work "tours". Given the high turnover figures for new employees, due to the "induction crisis", it thus becomes economically sound to put more effort into the selection process. Secondly, it is important to maintain a high level of stability among crews working as a cohesive team. Frequent changes of personnel are disruptive to working relationships that already must exist within a delicate balance, because of the actual working conditions and the severe environmental pressures.

There is some indication that the image of the offshore worker has tempered from the adventurous, glamorous, get-rich-quick ideals of the early days of North Sea drilling, to the realities of an often arduous and routine job; be it in a rather unique or novel environment. It is therefore suggested that a more stable workforce is emerging (Norman & Brebner, 1985). Although this should ultimately reduce accidents, it has already been observed that it is not just the "new" personnel who have accidents offshore.

It is estimated that about 47,000 people are currently working offshore in the North Sea oil and gas extraction industry. Figures for the U.K. sector show a steady increase each year (Source: *Development of the Oil & Gas Resources of the United Kingdom*, H.M.S.O., 1985).

1981	21,000
1982	21,500
1983	28,700
1984	31,300

These figures include construction workers, personnel on mobile drilling rigs, service vessels and support barges and survey teams. The survey carried out on 30 September 1984 indicates that, on that day, 16,462 were offshore. This includes 14,002 U.K. personnel (85%) and 2,460 non-U.K. personnel. A total of 52 different nationalities were recorded, but in the main, the largest foreign representations were, Norway 27%, U.S.A. 18%, Spain 12.5% and Holland 9%. Although the offshore population in the Dutch sector is much smaller, i.e. estimated to be approximately 3,000+, and no figures exist to indicate the various nationalities employed, informed comment suggests that it is also a very cosmopolitan environment. The degree to which this may present additional problems to working in the offshore environment needs to be assessed, for example; the extent to which a cosmopolitan living and working environment is a source of stimulation or distress and how language difficulties and cultural differences affect team working essential for maximum performance and personal safety.

Occupational stress is responsible in part for deterioration in both physiological and psychological health; it may also be an important factor to consider in the incidence of accidents offshore in the North Sea oil and gas extraction industry, in what is an already acknowledged hazardous; arduous and severe working environment. The effects of stressors may contribute to high labour turnover rates and, in addition to the cost incurred, may also have a detrimental effect on working relationships in a cosmopolitan working environment that necessitates high levels of co-operation, trust and good communications. By providing information, insight, explanation and prescription, this study therefore seeks to raise the level of awareness for those individuals at risk, and among those that have the power to make changes to improve the quality of working life.

This investigation therefore aims to promote both an increased level of awareness on this issue of occupational stress and the development of some expertise, which may lead to theoretical and practical problem solving. The positive benefits could be greater productivity and increased job satisfaction, with minimal costs in terms of ill health and well being of the individual.

3 Literature review

The extraction of gas and oil from the North Sea has, in the past 30 years, generated more than passing news. Boom-town euphoria and get rich quick tales have been tempered with the sobering realisation of some of the costs to be paid when tragedy strikes and lives are lost. For example, the *Sea Gem* disaster in 1965, the loss of the *Alexander Kjelland* in 1981 and the *Ocean Ranger* in 1982 (a total loss of 226 lives). It is perhaps not possible to put real and meaningful costs on these losses nor on the others claimed, since the operations began in the North Sea in the mid 1960s; but however it is calculated, it may only be "tip-of-the-iceberg" costs to the industry when one considers the full financial burden of occupational stressors or distress in the environment. Here, mismanaged stress is seen as the insidious factor which plays a part in the deterioration of physiological and psychological health; the underlying cause of many accidents offshore; and having a negative effect on productivity when working relationships and morale break down in a situation where co-operation and successful teamwork are the vital elements of a safe and efficient working environment.

It was therefore surprising to discover that very little is known about this aspect of life and working conditions of the individuals working in this unique environment on offshore drilling rigs and production platforms. A computer based, information retrieval search into both social science and medical files indicates minimal investigation into this topic, and most of the literature is of a purely descriptive and sometimes anecdotal nature. With the exception of a study in Norway (Sunde, 1983) even the relatively recent symposium on safety and health in the oil and gas extraction industries (Luxembourg, 1983) was restricted to descriptive accounts of the physical and psychological risks to health as a result of working and living conditions offshore.

Until the mid 1970s the research was of a technical nature; for example, Attfield (1974), "How Safe are North Sea Platforms?"; and unfortunately often the result of learning from costly mistakes. The major concern in these times was to improve or change technology and systems to meet the demands of the difficult and unrelenting North Sea.

It is a tribute to the design of structures and systems currently used that accident rates and fatalities actually have stabilised when one considers the annual increase in personnel employed offshore. But these measures are not in themselves complete; the safety of offshore workers is inexorably linked to health when one considers such factors as mental well being and morale. Thus it was a slow but natural progression to direct the focus of attention from the "hardware", i.e. the technology of the offshore scene to the "software" (Sunde, 1985); that is the thousands of people employed in the many and varied offshore occupations.

However, this early research, for example Ross (1975) "Noise on Offshore Platforms", still has a clearly "ergonomic" emphasis. Noise is indicated as a factor in the deterioration of physical health, due maybe to sleeplessness or irritation; and in operational safety because of speech interference and the possibility of misunderstood verbal communication.

Exposure to excessive noise, that is approximately 80 decibels, on a recurring, prolonged basis can cause stress (Ivancevich & Matteson, 1980) and temporary or permanent hearing loss, if inadequate ear protection is not used. The following table (3.1) is an indication of the range of noise levels measured in the vicinity of the main machinery on a number of offshore platforms.

Table 3.1 Range of noise levels for main machinery areas of offshore installations

	Noise Range dB(A)
Water Injection Pump Houses	103 – 109
Generator Houses	85 – 96
Well Bays	72 – 90
Shipping Pump Areas	86 – 94
Reciprocating Compressor Houses	80 – 99

Source: Ross, 1978

Noise levels are similar to those found in comparable onshore locations, but close proximity of a number of such sources on platforms will give high background levels. This is illustrated by the noise levels found in recreation and living areas (Table 3.2).

￮ᶠ **noise levels in accommodation and recreational**

	Noise Range dB(A)
Lunchrooms and Kitchens	62 - 74
Bunk Houses	50 - 72
Toolpushers Office	64 - 72
Radio Rooms	62 - 77

Source: Ross (1978)

Noise levels are rated high compared with similar onshore based locations and are at least 5 dB(A) higher than the habitability standards recommended by certain European countries for merchant ships (Hoyland, 1976). On these grounds recommendations are made regarding the future design and layout of installations. The International Symposium on Safety and Health in the oil and gas extraction industry (April 1983, Luxembourg) continued to raise this issue of noise as a hazard in the offshore working environment (Boucheny, 1983: Bustin, 1983) and the need to solve many of the problems at the design stage. This also includes other physical aspects of the environment, such as vibration and ventilation in living accommodation. But although the assumption is made that "noise" is a stressor in the environment which makes demands on the individual, no attempt is made to explain why one individual suffers ill health, or has an accident despite the use of ear defenders and optimised design to reduce background noise in living accommodation, yet another individual copes and thrives. It is not sufficient to consider only the "hardware" in trying to solve the problems; the "software" must be addressed also in terms of individual characteristics and differences. Kummer (1983) reminds us that, although noise levels can be expressed in objective, and physical terms, reaction to noise is a subjective issue.

Frère (1975) appears to be the first to acknowledge this point, but the study is limited to a purely descriptive anecdotal account, based on his personal working experience as a physician on board a pipe laying barge in the North Sea, which was also involved in some of the early drilling rig and production platform construction. Although the main aim was to identify some of the health conditions and medical problems associated with severe environmental situations it also indicated the hazardous nature of the work due to high winds, rolling seas, extreme cold and noise; and brings attention to the existence of sources of psychological stress and safety problems for the individual exposed to crowded and noisy sleeping accommodation.

Another paper based on the same study, Philbert, Frère & Emmanueli (1975) is still in the descriptive style, but it also raises the issue of the potential problems of a heterogeneous population, living and working in confined conditions for long periods of time; factors such as disparity in status according to nationality and/or category of work performed, and lack of project goal information are suggested. Other issues are identified as contributing to psychological problems, and ultimately non-adaptation to the life-style; for example, worker inexperience and lack of pre-screening of employees. It was therefore suggested that legislation be set down to maintain some control on the recruitment of those employed on board these vessels and the conditions in which they work.

Although this working environment of a pipe-laying barge is acknowledged as part of the oil and gas extraction industry there are however slight differences in offshore working that should be made clear at this point, and acknowledged in the event of finding differences between the workers on a pipe-laying barge and workers on production platforms and/or drilling rigs. First, it is common practice to work for much longer periods offshore; Frère reports a pattern of two and one half months on the barge, with one month rest period in between; although some nationalities may sign-on and stay for much longer periods, because they do not intend to travel home on their time off period and also want to avoid paying hotel bills. Secondly, the barge does move around, be it sometimes very slowly, it is going "somewhere" just like a ship, whereas production platforms do not, neither do drilling rigs, except for location changes when most personnel are taken off the rig anyway. In this respect oil barge workers are more like seafarers, and may not therefore be directly comparable to the offshore workers on production platforms and drilling rigs. (It may also be that significant differences are observed between drilling and production crews anyway.)

This theme of finding "suitable" people was the focus of a report based on an investigation by the Petroleum Industry Training Board (P.I.T.B.) (Livy & Vant, 1979). They state that one of the key problems for the offshore industry has been selecting the right people ... " the life is not for everyone". The study focused on the jobs of "roustabout" and "roughneck"; major categories of workers at the unskilled and semi-skilled manual level; and investigated selection criteria and thus predictors of those people who will stay a long time and work hard and well in arduous, dangerous and socially isolating conditions. Livy & Vant emphasise the importance of maintaining fully manned and stable work crews.

Disruption to working relationships, caused by constantly changing personnel, is acknowledged as a contributory factor in the deterioration of morale, unsatisfactory productivity levels and, ultimately, safety consciousness suffers. In fact, "teamwork" was rated highest by the participants of the study, as the quality necessary for the job, closely followed by "physical fitness". Both "stayers" and "leavers" of this offshore work were questioned about offshore life, their likes and dislikes, and it was found that "work itself" was a major cause of job satisfaction and a factor in retaining motivated employees. Those who had gone offshore for mainly financial reasons, e.g. because they had been unemployed, were most likely to leave. Yet, the main reasons for leaving were shift work and difficulties with home life. A new selection procedure was established on the basis of this investigation, which also included a training course and a follow-up assessment. Key criteria such as teamwork ability and physical aptitude were included in practical, situational, leaderless group tasks but the focus appears to be mainly on the individual, without taking into account the interactive element of family and work issues. It is likely that screening should be extended to identify mental wellbeing and include an assessment of issues such as "social support" and stability of home/family background. It is thus necessary to consider the individual's suitability in terms of the inter-active product of private and career worlds.

Selection procedures to identify "suitable" personnel for offshore work are vital, but it is also necessary to know what effects the working environment is having, both in the short and long term. Having selected the possible "best" individuals it is important to know the characteristics of the person showing signs of impaired health, or those who may be at particular risk of accident and injury; and to understand the conditions and danger that they are exposed to in order to minimise and control any potentially harmful effects. (Here it should be acknowledged that lack of stimulation, boredom, lack of job clarity and uncertain future goals are also viewed as potential "hazards" for the offshore worker.) Recent papers, Prossin (1983), Roythorne (1983) and Elliott (1985) are aimed at helping physicians, with patients working in the offshore environment, cope with the physical problems that may arise, the specialised treatments needed and the requirements for assessing fitness for work in an isolated environment. Again, these accounts are of a descriptive nature intending to familiarise doctors with the life and working conditions offshore, i.e. climatic conditions, mechanical and electrical hazards, exposure to harmful substances, the effects of exposure to noise, vibration, ionising radiation, inadequate lighting and fire and explosion hazards. It is also important for a doctor to be able to diagnose a patient "fit" for the demands of offshore working without risk of him being a danger to himself or others working with him. Prossin (1983) briefly comments on psychological stress and refers to the factor of isolation and the effect this may have on morale, mental wellbeing and, ultimately, safety. Complaints of fatigue, insomnia and inadaptability are once more identified as potential stressors in the environment. The working hours, the effects of shift work, adequate rest periods and shore leave all are seen as having a significant impact on the relationship between the worker, his working environment, his family and his social relationships (Prossin, 1983).

It is also suggested that injuries during working hours may be determined by these stressors in the occupational environment. Although Prossin is mainly concerned with physical wellbeing, for the first time "quality of working life" is discussed with regard to the offshore worker, and the need to consider the interactive efforts of work, the family and social relationships when assessing potential psychosocial factors of offshore working. However, the concluding advice given to physicians on "pre-placement examinations", i.e. "contraindications to offshore work", still refer only to the physical condition of the individual, and make no mention of morale or mental wellbeing which may be dictated or influenced by the particular "life stage" of the person (i.e. family and social relationships).

The literature discussed so far pertains only to "men" at work offshore. Traditionally the industry projects a "male" image and even after 30 years of North Sea operations it remains essentially a "man's world".

An investigation commissioned by the Equal Opportunities Commission (Moore & Wybrow, 1984) indicates that the Norwegian sector of the North Sea has been the only area to successfully employ women offshore in a wide range of jobs. In 1983, 588 women workers were recorded of the total offshore population of 15,340 (3.8%); the majority working in catering, as nurses, medics, or in administrative functions. Although some women are employed as geologists, radio operators and roustabouts, the jobs are in the main confined to what is considered "women's work" and therefore job discrimination on the grounds of sex is evident. It is however believed that women will take an ever increasing role in offshore working, but the change in culture will be a slow one. Yet, compared to the progress of women working offshore in the U.K. and Dutch sectors of the North Sea, this would seem a veritable explosion.

Moore & Wybrow describe their difficulty in finding available statistics for women working offshore in the U.K. sector and conclude that the best, and probably generous, estimate would be less than 0.5% (1981–82 total U.K. offshore population approximately 21–22,000). It was believed that about 25 women were working offshore on a regular normal shift basis as geologists, petroleum engineers, structural engineers and administrative assistants, and it was observed that a few more women went offshore for brief, and occasional visits as part of their work. The report concludes that there is evidence of widespread, almost universal, discrimination against women employed in the British sector of the North Sea oil industry and there is no indication that any significant change will take place in the near future. It is therefore not surprising that this investigation, restricted to U.K. and Dutch sector offshore workers, is limited to an all male population. The research presently being conducted in Norway (Sunde, 1983; Hellesøy, 1985) is however an indication of some of the stress problems that may be specific to women offshore and the issues that are raised by their presence in the micro society of the offshore environment. The relevance of the report to this investigation will be discussed later, together with the work of Hellesøy in Norway.

The role of women and offshore working is discussed again in a paper presented at the International Rig Medics Conference (Aberdeen, June 1985). This time however it is about the wives of the men who work offshore and the existence of stress related problems caused by "absent" husbands and the frequent and recurring partings and reunions (Morrice, 1985). This suggestion is supported by Hellesøy's work in the Norwegian sector, i.e. that the most commonly reported problems in relation to family life were problems related to "leaving home" for offshore work. Morrice's study, which compares wives with offshore husbands with wives with non-offshore working husbands, is relevant to this investigation in three ways.

First, it again highlights the need to take into account the interactive element of work, work relationships and family and social relationships in assessing psychosocial and occupational factors of offshore working. As Livy & Vant (1979) suggest, "difficulties with home life" was one of the main reasons reported by roustabouts and roughnecks for leaving offshore work. Secondly, as Morrice states, husbands working offshore may "mirror" this stress related syndrome in the form of the "Intermittent Wife Syndrome" with the consistent triad of symptoms namely, anxiety, depression and sexual difficulties; and so there is a need to know the extent to which this is a potential stressor in the environment. Finally, not only is it an element of concern that the wives of offshore workers may be more likely to suffer a deterioration in health because of the lifestyle that they lead, but it is also unsatisfactory in that this may render them incapable of providing the social support which could mitigate some of the effects of potential stressors in their husbands' working environment. Lack of social support in the home situation may compound any stress problems (Sunde, 1983).

However, there is another side to this issue that is so far overlooked, in that "work" may be viewed as a vital part of the process of coping with "life stress". Work imposes meaning and structure to life; through work an individual establishes a sense of identity. But perhaps for many it is also a source of refuge against life stress, and work may provide a "psychological haven" (Maclean, 1979) against problems and depression that may result from loneliness or difficult and demanding family and social relationships that do not offer any psychological or emotional support. It is therefore necessary to differentiate between those that perceive offshore work as this means of "escape", and those who may possibly be more likely to suffer "a double blow" from the consequences of stress, because the work environment does not offer the individual a chance to cope with non-work stress by burying himself in work.

The investigation reported by Sunde (1983) is the most detailed work available on the psychosocial aspects of offshore work. It is an on-going research project which evolved from a sociological study of the personnel on the Statfjord Platforms in the Norwegian sector of the North Sea and began in 1979 at the Research Centre for Occupational Health and Safety, University of Bergen. It is sponsored by Mobil Exploration Norway Incorporated.

Although the results from the full investigation have not been published, some of the details of the initial investigation are available (Hellesøy, 1985). Some information has also been released to the Norwegian Directorate of Health and was presented in a paper by the Chief Medical Officer, Dr Sunde, at the International Symposium on Safety & Health in the Oil & Gas Extraction Industries, Luxembourg, 1983. Demographic characteristics of the offshore population are dealt with in great detail because they are recognised as important indices in some measurements of health (Gogstad, Hellesøy & Eide, 1981; Sunde, 1983).

Also an attempt is made to identify potentially negative and positive factors in the offshore environment. Satisfaction and dissatisfaction with work, living conditions and transportation is recorded and analysed in terms of level of mental strain reported, and for emotional difficulties such as agitation, depression and isolation. Relationships between dissatisfaction with living conditions and indicators of mental strain quite clearly persist. Patterns are different for each type of emotional problem, though all display strong associations with noise and lack of privacy. Other aspects of offshore life, such as job satisfaction, physical environment, safety and experience of risk, have also been examined in relationship to health indicators. The study is important in that it recognises the need to acknowledge the interaction of home and family when considering the psychosocial factors of offshore working, and it produces quantitative data to support some of the earlier descriptive accounts of life and working conditions offshore.

This offshore population is a relatively young one, the majority being in the 25–30 age group, and Sunde (1983) suggests that perhaps this factor reflects the lack of research, i.e. nobody has found it worthwhile to study a presumably young, healthy population. But the fact is that the people in this age group are most likely to be in the midst of establishing a family, or disrupting one; and it is perhaps the period of greatest financial strain.

Hellesøy (1985) also believes that there is a need to investigate the possible long term effects of continuous exposure to different potential sources of stress in the offshore environment. Questions such as, "When, if ever, is the oil worker going to be burned out?", "Will there be an increased rate of heart infarction or other diseases over the years?". He also points out, however, that many differences in response were found between the subgroups of the study (the divisions used were, operational personnel, catering personnel, drillers and flotell crews) and, although certain general findings are reported, there is here a warning that a global approach is not adequate, and that further work should be aimed at specific work groups and with greater attention focused on the individual.

Although there is no reason to believe that there are any great differences between the offshore workers in the Norwegian sector and the U.K. and Dutch sectors, there are two issues that may be important and relevant to any differences in findings.

First, the "Norwegianisation" of the Norwegian sector has meant that the population is much less heterogeneous than it was in the early 1970s and is certainly less so than the current U.K. and Dutch sectors. The September 1984 U.K. survey reveals the presence of 52 different nationalities, in addition to the U.K. personnel offshore on the day (16,462 employees offshore; 14,002 U.K. personnel; 2,460 non-U.K. personnel). The extent to which the differences in work experience, language and cultural background may be a source of distress or stimulation in the offshore environment is not yet known, but the catastrophe to follow the oil industry, predicted by sociologists in Norway in the early 1970s, has not occurred partly, suggests Sunde (1983), because the offshore population is less heterogeneous. It was predicted that an unhealthy environment would exist, characterised by broken families, extensive alcoholism, drug abuse and psychological disturbance.

Secondly, the extent to which the presence of women working offshore has an effect on the psychosocial and occupational aspects of working and living on drilling rigs and production platforms is not known. It is reasonable to assume that some differences will be observed and the present Norwegian research programme may eventually report on this. Meanwhile, a quote from the Moore & Wybrow paper gives some indication of the potential difference. The O.I.M. described the situation thus "...the first thing that hits you when you get off the chopper, when there are women on the rig, is the smell of aftershave".

It is therefore very evident that quantitative data on the sources of stress in the offshore oil industry are minimal, and at present confined to the Norwegian sector, which may be "different" in the ways described. Thus, the aim of this study is to investigate the psychological and occupational aspects of offshore working on drilling rigs and production platforms in the U.K. and Dutch sectors of the North Sea, with an all male sample of subjects to provide quantitative data on the sources of stress in this unique working environment.

Four-fifths of the earth's surface is covered by water. It is therefore most probable that the oil and gas supplies of the future will come from sub-sea reservoirs, in ever more hostile environments. What is happening in European waters today will serve as a technological forerunner for the rest of the world tomorrow (A. E. Bennett opening address to the Commission of the European Communities International Symposium on Safety & Health in the Oil & Gas Extraction Industries, Luxembourg, April 1983). "No society has the right to require that any group of workers be exposed to abnormal risks to health and safety, even when it is a question of producing essential supplies such as energy." It is therefore an important and vital first step that risks, both in the short and long term, be identified and quantified.

4 What is stress?

As already stated in the Introduction, to understand the phenomena of stress at work it is necessary to define, identify, measure and thereby optimise stress levels to enable an individual to realise personal and organisational goals. Before describing the methodology used in this study, that seeks to identify and measure sources of stress among offshore workers in the oil and gas extraction industry, it is therefore necessary to define the concept under investigation.

Many authors have offered definitions of the term "stress" and as Beehr & Newman (1978) suggest there really is no universally agreed meaning among behavioural scientists, nor scientists in general. To understand why different conceptual approaches exist on the nature of stress it is important to be aware of the origins of the study of stress and how the contemporary view of stress as an interactive process has evolved.

THE HISTORICAL PERSPECTIVE

The suggestion that emotional stress might be a major cause of ischaemic heart disease was proposed as early as 1860 by Claude Bernard, but it was still a rare disease at this time. However, by 1910, an observation of the high incidence of angina pectoris among Jewish members of the business community was attributed in part to a hectic pace of life (Osler, 1910). This appears to be the first link suggested between new patterns of physical and mental disorder, and urban living with increasing population densities. Thus, "living an intense life" which taxed the nervous energy of the Jew to the uttermost, "the system is subjected to stress and strain which seems to be a basic factor in so many cases of angina pectoris" (Osler, 1910).

Yet it is Hans Selye, a medical student of the 1930s and 1940s, who is the generally acknowledged "father of stress". His interest focused on the notion that all patients, whatever the disease, "looked and felt sick". That is, they show nonspecific manifestations of disease, "a stereotyped syndrome of being sick" (Selye, 1956). Through subsequent experimental work on both animals and humans, Selye tried to explain the process of stress related illness and identified the predictable sequence of response which he called the "general adaptation syndrome theory" (G.A.S.). This consists of three stages that the individual will encounter in a stressful situation. The alarm reaction is the immediate psychophysiological response when the "initial shock phase" of lowered resistance is immediately followed by the "countershock phase", during which the individual's defence mechanisms become active. Cannon (1932) defined this as the "emergency reaction", that is, a fight or flight response. Components of this response include increased heart rate, rapid breathing, increased blood pressure, increased alertness and feelings of nervousness. The second stage, "resistance" is the stage of maximum adaptation and return to equilibrium for the individual. But if the alarm reaction is elicited too intensely and too frequently over an extended period without an effective outlet, or defence mechanisms do not work, then the third stage of the syndrome is reached, "exhaustion", when the adaptive mechanisms collapse. Selye (1983) points out that resistance does not go on indefinitely once the adaptation stage is reached, even when given sufficient energy, because the "human machine" eventually becomes the victim of "wear and tear". At this stage of exhaustion the negative, destructive consequences of stress become manifest. Selye (1983) believes that rest and sleep can restore resistance and adaptability following exhaustion, as a result of excessively stressful activity, but that complete restoration is probably impossible. He says, "every biological activity causes wear and tear, it leaves some irreversible 'chemical scars' which accumulate to constitute signs of ageing" (Selye, 1983).

Thus the term "stress" has its origins in the field of medicine. Within this view of stress the understanding is in terms of a stimulus-response model (S-R), as illustrated in Figure 4.1, and many definitions encapsulate the concept of stress in this manner.

However, a simple energy-exchange or stimulus-response model of stress is not adequate in the understanding of the phenomena of stress. There is a need to consider the interactive effect between the stress stimulus and individual concerned. Caplan (1964) adopts an "interactive-process" viewpoint by incorporating the S-R model and an understanding of the organism within the principles of homeostasis. This is the co-ordination of physiological processes which maintain a steady state in the organism (Cannon, 1935). It is the staying power of the body in an ever-changing environment. Natural homeostatic mechanisms normally maintain a state of resistance but are not able to cope with unusually

Figure 4.1 Stimulus-response model of stress

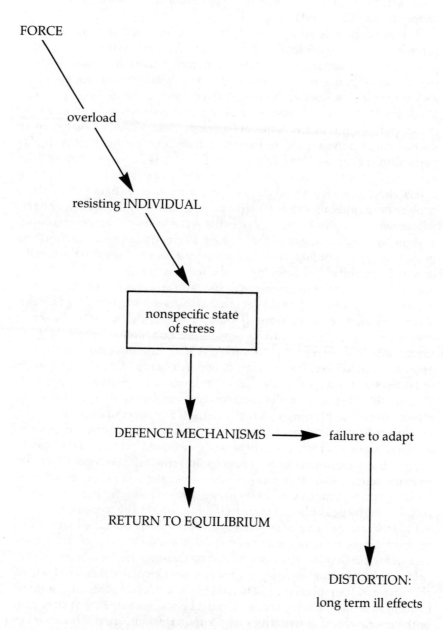

Source: C. L. Cooper (1981), *The Stress Check*, p.7

heavy demands that may arise from physical, psychological and/or sociocultural demands. Under homeostatic principles there is a finite supply to meet demands.

Others adopt this view of stress as an "interactive process" without reference to a physiological model, but suggest that the cognitive processes of the organism must be taken into account in the understanding of the response to a stressful situation. Thus perception, appraisal and judgement of the situation is all important (Cofer & Appley, 1964). McGrath (1976) said, "...there is a potential for stress when an environmental situation is perceived as presenting a demand which threatens to exceed the person's capabilities and resources for meeting it ...". A similar definition is proposed by Lazarus (1971) which is also a reminder of the very wide scope of the problem under investigation. He says, "Stress refers then to a very broad class of problems differentiated from other problem areas because it deals with any demands which tax the system, whatever it is, a physiological system, a social system, or a psychological system, and the response of that system ... reaction depends on how the person interprets or appraises (consciously or unconsciously) the significance of a harmful, threatening or challenging event".

It is suggested that the systematic focus on stress in organisations has, in part, been prevented by the fact that stress seems to be related to such a large number of conditions (House, 1974(b); Selye, 1973; Beehr & Newman, 1978). "It is too all encompassing a phenomenon, too large to investigate" (Schuler, 1980). Awareness that "cognitive appraisal" is an essentially individual-based affair (Cooper, 1981) and that investigation must be in terms of a person's "vulnerability profile" (Appley & Trumbull, 1976) adds to the complexity of understanding this issue of stress. Beehr & Newman (1978) attempt to conceptualise job stress, employee health and organisational effectiveness in terms of a facet analysis model, which they suggest is designed to delimit and make explicit the phenomena one wishes to investigate. The model includes environment, personal, process, human consequences, organisational consequences, adaptive response, and time as facets, each of which includes many possible elements that might need to be considered. Table 4.1 is an example of some of the suggestions made for the personal and process facets, and is an indication of the complexity of the stress research situation in terms of an "interactive-process" model.

However, another important concept must also be considered within this historical perspective, and is vital to the understanding of the stress concept as an interactive process. It must be acknowledged that stress has both beneficial and destructive effects upon the individual. This assumption is based on the model proposed by Yerkes & Dodson (1908). The

"Yerkes-Dodson Law", the "inverted U" hypothesis, states that performance improves with increasing amounts of stress to a certain optimum
point, but beyond this a deterioration in performance will be observed.
Thus, too little stress may be as bad as too much. Selye (1956) supports
this idea with his physiological concept of stress. He states, "no-one can
live without experiencing some degree of stress all the time ... any
activity or emotion causes stress". He defines biological stress as a nonspecific bodily response to any demand, not necessarily a response to
excessive demands.

Table 4.1 Facets of job stress and types of elements

Personal Facet

(a) Psychological condition (personality traits and
behavioural characteristics)

- Type A
- ego needs
- need for clarity/intolerance
  for ambiguity
- introversion/extraversion
- internality/externality
- approval seeking
- defensiveness
- intelligence
- abilities
- previous experience with
  stress
- impatience
- intrapersonal conflicts
- self esteem
- motives/goals/aspirations
- typical anxiety level
- perceptual style
- values (human, religious
  etc.)
- personal work standards
- need for perfection
- satisfaction with job and
  other major aspects of
  life

(b) Physical Condition

- physical fitness/health
- diet and eating habits
- exercise, work, sleep and relaxation patterns

(c) Life Stage Characteristics

- human development stages
- family stages
- career stages

cont'd

Table 4.1 cont'd

    (d) Demographics

- age
- education (amount and type)
- sex
- race
- socio-economic status
- occupation, avocation

Process Facet

    (a) Psychological Processes

- perceptions (of past, present and predicted future situations)
- evaluation of situation
- response selection
- response execution

    (b) Physical Processes

- physiological, biological
- neurological
- chemical

Source: Beehr & Newman (1978), pp. 671-672

The concept is therefore critical to the understanding that demand must be considered in relation to "too much", and "too little", and this is the basis of the "person-environment fit" approach to understanding stress at work (Van Harrison, 1975; French, 1973). Assessment of fit or misfit is in terms of the desired and actual levels of, for example, work complexity, responsibility, workload etc. Therefore, two types of stress may exist. Either "demands" (for example, skill or ability) which the individual cannot meet, or insufficient "supplies" to meet for his needs. Job stress is conceptualised as a misfit of either of these relationships between the individual and the job environment. Schuler (1980) suggests the weakness of the fit/misfit model is that it implies that an individual in a situation of "fit" is without stress (a state of death according to Selye) although at maximum satisfaction. But this criticism does not stand if one acknowledges that "fit" is not a "once-and-for-all" static situation. State of fit and misfit is a continually changing dynamic process, and any assessment made is only with the purpose of reducing some of the potential sources of stress in the environment.

Figure 4.2 The person–environment model of stress

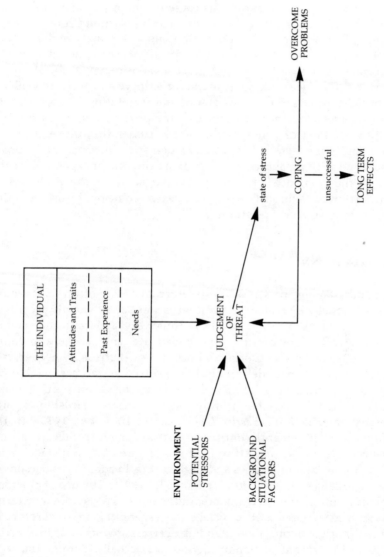

Source: C. L. Cooper (1981), *The Stress Check*, p. 10.

The model shown in Figure 4.2 therefore conceptualises the notion of stress in terms of person-environment fit. The model does not assume that a return to the preceding steady state is the only beneficial outcome possible as hypothesised under homeostatic principles, and so it acknowledges that a state of stress may be a stimulus to growth and development. The concept of stress only makes sense when seen as an imbalance in the context of an individual-environment transaction (Cooper, 1981).

Although this approach to understanding stress has common-sense appeal, it poses yet more problems for the researcher, in that the "subjective" response to demand must be considered, and not only a purely objective measure. Some individuals thrive and perform well in a situation that others find overwhelming and debilitating. Thus, McGrath (1970) suggests, "we need to approach the problems of stress systematically with a set of concepts that encompasses the full sequence of events (objective demand, subjective demand, response and consequence) and with an approach aimed at seeking the linkages among the parts of the sequence". He suggests that some of the problems of identification of "subjective load" may be overcome by the use of multi-stressor, multi-effect type studies.

DEFINITIONS

The understanding of stress is therefore in terms of an "interactive process" model which is not a static situation but a dynamic process in which time plays a vital role. It is thus very apparent that simple dictionary definitions of stress are inadequate when seeking to define and conceptualise psychosocial and occupational stress. However, it is observed that dictionary definitions have evolved to embrace the changes in the use of the expression. For example, in the seventeenth century "stress" (derived from Latin) was used to mean "hardship, straits, adversity or affliction" (*Shorter Oxford English Dictionary*, 1933). In the eighteenth and nineteenth centuries, the use changed to indicate "strain, pressure, force or strong effort". This was intended to include terms relating to the laws of physics and engineering, in addition to persons or person's organs or mental powers (Hinckle, 1973). The use of the term within the field of physics to understand an object's resistance to external pressure was adopted by the social sciences, and this may therefore be seen as the origin of our understanding of stress at work as an interactive process. Most recent dictionary definitions actually identify the term "stress" with disease, "suffered by managers etc., subjected to continual stress" (*Concise Oxford Dictionary*, New Edition, 1984).

~~ver, for the purpose of this investigation into psychosocial and
sources of stress, the definition and conceptualisation
Beehr & Newman (1978) might be appropriate. "Job stress
:uation wherein job-related factors interact with a worker to
change (i.e. disrupt or enhance) his or her psychological and/or physiological condition such that the person (i.e. mind-body) is forced to deviate
from normal functioning. This definition also serves to define what we
mean by 'employee health'; namely, a person's mental and physical
condition. We are referring to health in its broadest sense — the complete
continuum from superb mental and physical health all the way to death.
Note that we are not excluding the possibility of beneficial effects of
stress on health." (Beehr & Newman, 1978, p. 670).

SYMPTOMS OR OUTCOMES OF STRESS

These may be classified within the headings suggested by Beehr &
Newman, "the human consequences facet", with manifestations of stress
at three levels, that is psychological, behavioural and physical; and the
"organisational consequences facet". Table 4.2 indicates some of the
elements proposed within each of these dimensions, some of which have
been empirically studied within the context of job-stress and employee
health.

Table 4.2 Facets of job stress and types of elements

Human Consequences Facet

(a) Psychological Health Consequences

- anxiety, tension
- depression
- dissatisfaction, boredom
  somatic complaints
- loss of concentration
- repression, suppression
  of feelings and ideas

- psychological fatigue
- feelings of futility, low
  self esteem and inadequacy
- feelings of alienation
- psychosis
- anger

cont'd

Table 4.2 cont'd

(b) Physical Health Consequences

- cardiovascular disease
- gastrointestinal disorders
- respiratory problems
- cancer
- arthritis
- death

- headaches
- skin disorders
- bodily injuries
- physical/physiological fatigue or strain

(c) Behavioural Consequences

- dispensary visits
- drug use and abuse
- over or under eating
- nervous gesturing, pacing
- suicide or attempted suicide
- poor interpersonal relations (with family, friends, co-workers)

- risky behaviour (e.g. reckless driving, gambling)
- aggression
- vandalism
- stealing

Organisational Consequences

- changes in quantity, quality of job performance
- increase or decrease in withdrawal behaviours (absenteeism turnover, early retirement)
- increase or decrease in control over environment
- changes in profits, sales, earnings
- changes in ability to recruit and retain quality employees
- changes in ability to obtain raw materials
- changes in innovation and creativity
- changes in quality of work life
- increase or decrease in employee strikes
- changes in level of influence of supervisors
- grievances

Source: Beehr & Newman (1978), pp. 672–673

Listing symptoms or outcomes in distinct categories may however be misleading in that it implies discrete occurrences, when in fact they may be highly interrelated (Schuler, 1980). Although it is acknowledged that stress may be a stimulus to growth and development, the implication is that mis-managed stress has undesirable consequences both in the short and long term situations. But Cooper (1981) indicates that the nature and probability of the causal relationship involved is complex. Many of the stress studies reported have used self-report data for measures of both "cause" and "effect" variables, and simple correlational analysis. It is also very difficult adequately to take into account all the intervening variables possibly involved, and correlation is not equivalent to causation. Use of multivariate forms of analysis and data from longitudinal studies will help to overcome these weaknesses. However, new evidence continues to support the basic assumption that experience of mismanaged stress is responsible directly or indirectly for mental and physical suffering to some detriment of the individual and the organisation. Some of these costs, in terms of loss to the individual and the organisation, have already been identified in Section 2, so it is now the task to attempt to identify these potential sources of stress among the offshore workers in the oil and gas extractive industry, as they interact with and affect the characteristics of this particular occupational group.

5 Stress—a research model

In the absence of a conceptual framework for the specific investigation of psychosocial and occupational stressors among blue-collar workers, the decision was made to adopt the model proposed for study of managerial and white collar stress (Cooper & Marshall, 1978), see Figure 5.1. This is considered appropriate in that:

(i)   It embraces the contemporary interactive view of stress and accepts that any attempt to minimise negative consequences and optimise stress in an organisation must take a multi-dimensional approach.

(ii) These situations or features of the environment are not seen as inherently stressful, but as a combination of the individual with his specific physiology, psychology, personality and unique characteristics, within the life circumstance of the individual and the particular situation or work environment. Although it is therefore important to regard the concept in holistic terms, it is not a static situation, but a constantly changing process. Kelly & Cooper (1981) suggest from their investigation of the steel industry, that identifying and dealing with stress among blue collar workers is as complicated in terms of analysis and solutions as white collar managerial situations of stress, and that problems are manifold and not discrete entities.

(iii) The factors incorporated into this conceptualisation were drawn from multi-disciplinary fields of research, for example, psychology, management science, medicine and sociology etc. This need for an inter-disciplinary approach to research has been emphasised by many workers in this area (Quick & Quick, 1979; McLean, 1979; Sunde, 1983).

(iv) Although this diagrammatic representation is drawn mainly from research into sources of managerial stress over a 10–15 year period, the "shop-floor" studies that do exist appear to indicate that factors incorporated within this model are applicable to the labour force as a whole (Cooper & Marshall, 1978).

The model thus consists of seven major categories of stress, six

Figure 5.1 Sources of managerial stress

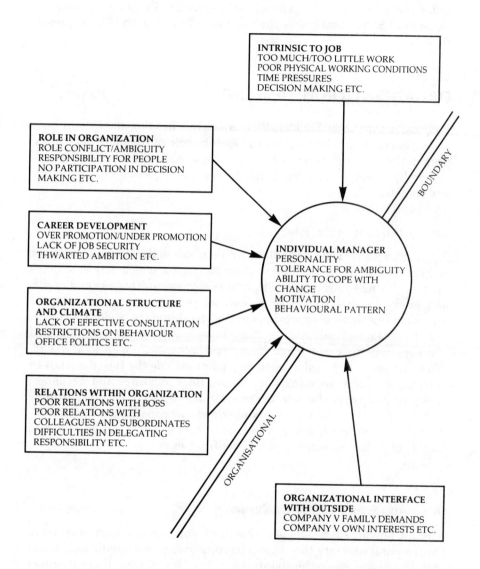

Source: Cooper, C. L. & Marshall, J. (1978), *Understanding Executive Stress.*

external and one internal, to the individual. These will be discussed in terms of the offshore worker in the oil and gas extraction industry in the following sections — Organisational Demands, Extra Organisational Sources of Stress, and finally the Individual Response and Consequence of Stress.

ORGANISATIONAL DEMANDS

Five major categories are identified under this heading and include task and physical factors intrinsic to the job; the role of the individual in the organisation; relationships within the organisation and inter-personal demands; career development; and finally, the organisational structure and climate.

Factors intrinsic to the Job

This includes the "task" and "physical" demands of the job of the offshore worker on drilling rigs and production platforms, which may be sources of stress in the environment. Physical environmental factors and health and safety factors, as stressors, featured prominently in the study of stress among blue-collar workers in the steel industry (Kelly & Cooper, 1981) and factors intrinsic to the job were a first and vital focus of investigation for early "shop-floor" researchers (Cooper & Marshall, 1978). Issues to be considered at this point include the task demands of working of shifts; working long hours; time pressures and deadlines; travel to and from the job; experience of risk; keeping up with new technology and equipment; work overload/underload; the physical conditions of heat, cold, noise, vibration etc.; the living conditions; and factors of isolation, restriction and confinement.

Task demands

(i)   SHIFT WORK: NIGHT WORKING

Monk & Folkard (1983) suggest that shift working is a common aspect of contemporary society that has to be consciously coped with and should thus be considered a potential stressor. They believe that there are three factors which have to be "got right" for successful coping with shift work namely; sleep, social and family life and circadian rhythms; and that these factors are all interrelated so that a problem with one factor can negate the positive effects of success achieved in the others.

The offshore worker is usually exposed to permanent and rapidly rotating shifts and disturbed sleep; he has a disrupted life pattern in that he does not return to a family home at the end of a working shift, and he must therefore remain in the constant company of his work peers, often in noisy living accommodation. In addition to these factors there is the extra disruption of the circadian rhythm pattern as a result of the constant changes caused by the unusual work schedule; that is, working only six months of the year on, for example, a 7 days on, 7 days off or a 14 days on, 14 days off routine. The extent to which these factors interact and mitigate potential stressors in the environment, or combine to resolve the "stress-chain" (Kelly & Cooper, 1983), is not known.

Although Selye (1976) suggests that individuals do habituate to shift work, and it becomes physically less stressful with time, the irregular work pattern of offshore working might prevent this habituation occurring. It is an issue that requires careful consideration with this particular group of workers. Disrupted sleep patterns can cause a deterioration in health and well being of the individual, which may in turn exacerbate other factors, for example, interpersonal relationships at work, efficiency and vulnerability to accidents as safety consciousness suffers.

(ii) LONG HOURS

In addition to a "shift" pattern of working, the actual number of hours worked offshore is long compared to onshore working. Usually a 12 hour shift is worked each day, with three breaks of 30 minutes each in the twelve hours. This continues every day without a break while the individual remains offshore (and can vary from 7 to 28 day tours, although 7 and 14 days is the most common arrangement in the North Sea). Research by Breslow & Buell (1960) points to a relationship between working long hours and coronary heart disease (C.H.D.) mortality. Their study of "light" industry in the U.S.A. found that subjects of less than 45 years of age, but working more than 48 hours per week, have twice the risk of death from C.H.D. compared with similar individuals working 40 hours or less a week. Also, a study of one hundred young coronary patients revealed that 25% of them had been working at two jobs, and an additional 40% worked for more than 60 hours or more a week (Russeck & Zohman, 1958). The offshore worker employed in what is rated as "heavy-industry" works 84 hours per week, and often for more than one week at a time but, although the offshore employee works these very long hours for several days at a time, they also have an equal number of days free time at home, completely away from the work environment.

Again, nothing is known about this unique work pattern, but perhaps adequate rest periods compensate for the long hours of work and negate any ill effects in the long term.

(iii)   TRAVEL TO AND FROM THE JOB

The factor of "travel" related to the job may also be a source of stress to consider for the offshore worker, and there are two different aspects to consider.

First, is the element of "time lost" from the free time period due to travelling long distances between home and the check-point for transportation to the rig or platform. It may also necessitate spending an extra night away from home in an hotel in order to be available for early morning crew-change helicopter flights. Generally, the more inaccessible the location is, the longer the offshore tours are likely to be, with equivalent time off to reduce time lost actually travelling to and from the installations.

Secondly, the "method" of transportation to and from the installation, normally by helicopter, may be perceived as an experience of risk, and thus a source of stress to the individual. Sunde (1983) indicates that this factor is the most common reason for resignation from offshore employment in the Norwegian sector of the North Sea. If weather conditions do not permit the use of helicopters for crew change operations then supply boats are used. This again means a time delay out of the individual's free time period, and necessitates being transferred from the installation to the boat via the personnel basket, which may be dangerous and difficult in the inclement weather conditions typical of the North Sea.

(iv)   EXPERIENCE OF RISK

This "experience of risk" factor could also extend to other elements in the environment, such as fear of fire, explosion, "blow-outs", falling objects, helicopter travel and severe weather conditions, including gale force winds and high seas. It is not known to what degree these special risks constitute sources of stress, or whether the continual emphasis on the need for safety concerning them, for example, safety training, the use of survival suits and the use of special protective equipment, is the greater source of stress. Bohemier (1985) quotes the example of a man who had been working offshore for 12 years and had never been in the water in his life, had avoided ever thinking about it and ever trying to familiarise himself with the hazards, equipment or procedures. He suggests that it is human nature to avoid thinking about danger or death, and this may be necessary to block out some of the realities of offshore work in order to face them every day.

Perceived adequacy of medical facilities and methods of coping with accidents or emergencies may also mitigate otherwise potential sources of stress in this hazardous environment. The degree to which the trained employee perceives the working environment as a dangerous place is important both in the short and long term consequences. In the short term it may increase vulnerability to accidents and thereby become a symptom and a consequence of stress; and in the long term it is necessary to consider the possible increased risk of coronary heart disease and circulatory disorders.

(v)   ADJUSTMENT TO NEW TECHNOLOGY

Another issue that may be important for this category of blue-collar worker is the degree to which technology changes in their environment and, therefore, the need to constantly become familiar with new equipment, systems and ways of working. The technology brought to the North Sea has, by necessity, radically changed to meet the demands of this difficult, deep water, environment, and as experience is gained, often from costly mistakes, changes are made. This rapidly changing situation may be a potential stressor (Toffler, 1970). Having a "boss" schooled in the "old ways" may be an extra burden for the new employee trained in the latest methods, and thus raises questions of adequacy of supervision, confidence and respect in the ability of those responsible for the efficient and safe operation of the installation, especially in an acknowledged hazardous environment where trust is a vital element to personal safety and where mistakes can have very serious consequences.

(vi)   WORK OVERLOAD/UNDERLOAD

The final aspect of the "task" factors intrinsic to the job to be considered is the issue of work overload, and work underload. This apparent paradox, of both too much and too little work being stressful, is explained in terms of the Yerkes-Dodson Law (Yerkes & Dodson, 1908), according to which there is a curvilinear relationship between the amount of work and health and performance (stress manifestation). Thus intermediate levels of work are optimal for health and performance. (See Figure 5.2, "the inverted-U hypothesis.)"

The main problem in dealing with this issue is one of individual

Figure 5.2 An expanded Yerkes-Dodson Curve

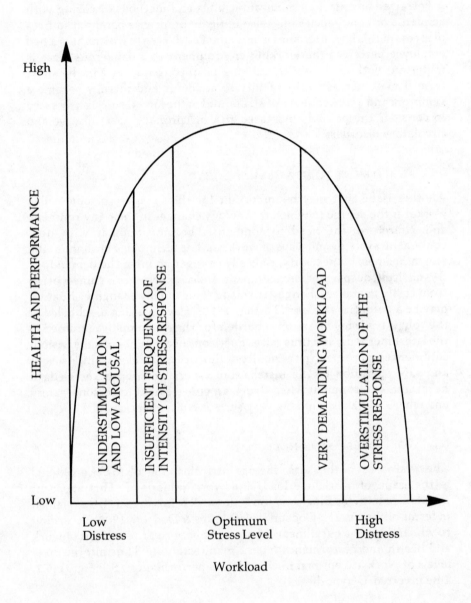

Source: Quick & Quick, 1979

differences in response to workload and workers vary greatly in their expectations, demands and coping with workload. Basically the problem has been investigated in two main ways, that is, making the distinction between quantitative and qualitative overload or underload (French & Caplan, 1973). Quantitative overload/underload results from the employee being given too many, too few tasks to complete in the time allowed; or it may be in the form of qualitative overload/underload when the individual does not feel able or capable to do the given task, or consequently that his potential or skills are not being utilised. French & Caplan (1970) found that objective quantitative overload was strongly linked to cigarette smoking, an important risk factor or symptom of C.H.D. Restriction of cigarette smoking behaviour offshore is limited to specific times during the 12 hour shift, and confined to special areas of the installation because of the risk of fire or explosion. This may compound the manifestation of stress in the environment if overload is of a quantitative nature.

Qualitative overload is frequently experienced by new, first time nursing supervisors who have been promoted on the basis of excellent clinical practice but who have no knowledge or skill of supervisory practices such as delegation or performance appraisal (Quick & Quick, 1979). Examples of this type of promotion through the ranks is also common practice in the oil and gas industry offshore and is thus a potential source of stress, which may be compounded in that an individual may find himself in the situation of taking disciplinary action with someone who has lived and worked alongside him as a peer in the past.

French & Caplan (1973) suggest that both qualitative and quantitative overload produces many different symptoms of psychological and physical strain; job dissatisfaction, job tension, lowered self esteem, threat, embarrassment, high cholesterol levels, increased heart rate, skin resistance and more cigarette smoking. Cooper & Marshall (1978) suggest that objective workload should not be viewed in isolation. It is relative to the individual's capacities and personality, thus the interactive relationship between the job and employee must not be overlooked.

"Underload" may be as damaging as overload, in that an individual is not given the opportunity to use his skills nor to develop to his full potential. Under-utilisation may lead to boredom, and "shifts" or lapse in attention, which are potentially serious in consequence while working in a dangerous environment for example, by reducing the individual's response to an emergency situation (Davidson & Veno, 1980). Underload as a result of lack of stimulation is potentially more damaging at night when the individual may have difficulty adjusting to the change in sleep pattern, but does not have enough work to keep himself alert (Poulton, 1978).

Work overload and underload may also result from irregular flows of work which are not under the control of the blue-collar worker; this would apply offshore where the pace can vary from very hectic to complete shutdown due to weather conditions. ("W.O.W." "waiting on weather" is a common enough term to warrant inclusion in the standard glossary of terms used by the industry: see Appendix I.)

Physical demands

The physical demands of offshore life are also important factors to consider under this heading of "factors intrinsic to the job", and two main areas of investigation exist. First, the actual physical conditions that the task is performed under and, secondly, that the installation also remains the living environment during the time spent offshore. Much has been written about the effects of working conditions of a particular job, for example, temperature (heat/cold), noise, vibration, lighting, colour, ventilation, cleanliness and diet, in relation to physical and mental health (Poulton, 1978; Ramsey, 1983; Jones, D., 1983; Gunderson, 1978). General acknowledgement of the hazards of physical conditions for the offshore worker is reported by the International Labour Office (1978) and within the papers presented to the International Symposium on Safety & Health in the Oil & Gas Extraction Industries, Luxembourg, April 1983.

Boucheny (1983) highlights "*noise*" as a contributory factor in the risk of an accident; Jones, C. (1983) suggests that "noise" offshore introduces two health hazards. First, the risk of occupational deafness, and secondly, that it causes a raised level of stress and may cause some psychological imbalance. Bustin (1983) suggests that many of the problems of noise and vibration may be solved at the design stage and evidence of earlier attempts to measure noise offshore exists (Ross, 1978), again mainly in the attempt to encourage improved design and construction. Kummer (1983) provides the reminder that although noise can be expressed in objective physical terms, it must be kept in mind that reaction to noise is a subjective experience. This issue of "noise" as a hazard in the physical environment appears to have been the main preoccupation with investigators of the offshore environment, with just reference to others purely in descriptive accounts (Frère, 1975; Philbert et al., 1975) of conditions offshore. Very little attempt has been made to investigate the physical demands of the offshore environment as sources of stress in a quantitative way or to consider the interactive or additive nature of them. The work of Hellesøy in Norway is the exception.

However, another factor (reported by Sunde, 1983) related to noise, but actually ignored in terms of investigation of psychosocial and occupation stressors, is that of *vibration*, which according to Selye (1976) is a very powerful stressor. Elevated catecholemines (adrenaline, noradrenaline and metabolites) is the recognised response to vibration. In the offshore environment vibration occurs as the result of rotary and/or impacting motion. For example, the presence of helicopters (especially as many installations have the heli-deck positioned over the living accommodation) and operations of driving pipe and "tripping" cause vibrations in the environment.

Many questions remain unanswered regarding the effects of the physical demands on the offshore worker, but it has been generally found that poor mental health of the industrial worker is directly related to unpleasant working conditions, the necessity to work fast, to expend a lot of physical effort and to excessive and inconvenient hours (Kornhauser, 1965). The degree to which the mental health of the offshore worker suffers under these conditions as stated by Kornhauser, and which would appear to be typical for some offshore occupations, is not known.

It is also necessary to consider the aspect of physical demands of the actual *living accommodation* offshore, and to what extent it constitutes as a potential source of stress in the environment. Factors may include problems associated with living in shared and confined conditions; lack of privacy, constant company, crowded sleeping quarters, inadequate recreation/leisure facilities. Dissatisfaction with these aspects of living conditions were some of the findings of the Norwegian Continental Shelf study recently conducted (Sunde, 1983, Hellesøy, 1985). However, there may be differences between the findings of the Norwegian investigations and the U.K. and Dutch sector study, in that the Norwegian sample includes women working offshore, and the population is much less heterogeneous since the "Norwegianisation" of the industry (Sunde, 1983). Most of the drilling rigs and production platforms in the U.K. and Dutch sectors of the North Sea are exclusively populated by male workers. The offshore oil and gas extraction industry traditionally projects a "male" image, and the presence of women in the environment is very limited and relatively new. The effects of this gradual change may themselves be a potential source of stress in the environment but, for this investigation, limited to a male population, the issue of working in an *exclusively male environment* will be examined as a possible stress factor of life offshore.

Paradoxically, although the individual working in this environment may lack privacy, and may virtually never be alone during the tour of duty, it is possible that feelings of *isolation* may persist and thus be a potential source of stress. Different factors may contribute to this. First, isolation caused by feelings of restriction or being confined to the rig or platform. Secondly, feelings of isolation from both his family/social relationships and from the outside world in general, especially if communications are restricted or delayed. Finally, the employee may experience isolation from his peers because he is required to wear ear protectors in the noisy environment for most of the 12 hour working shift, and is unable to engage in conversation with others (Kelly & Cooper, 1981).

Role demands

The role of the individual within the organisation is the second major category of potential stress at work. Role factors are related to behaviour expectation. The various behaviours expected of the individual by the different role senders in the environment are not always consistent or compatible and/or, it may be, that the individual does not in fact know what is expected of him or has insufficient information about the job or duties involved. These dysfunctions, identified as "role conflict" and role ambiguity respectively, have been extensively studied (Kahn *et al.*, 1964). The third factor to consider under this heading of role demands is that of "responsibility" for both "things" and people.

(i)   *Role Conflict*

This exists when an individual in his work environment is torn by conflicting job demands; doing things that he does not really want to do or does not believe are part of his job. Stress is caused by the inability or difficulty in meeting the various expectations (Van Sell *et al.*, 1981). Kahn, *et al.*, (1964) found that men who suffered more role conflict had lower job satisfaction and higher job related tension. French & Caplan (1970) demonstrated that role conflict was related to physiological stress. Their telemetry recordings of men at work in offices illustrated that heart rate was strongly related to the report of role conflict. Although it is not known to what degree the offshore worker may suffer from role conflict, there is potential for intersender conflict, for example, getting a job done to meet productivity needs or complying with the safety requirements. "Satisfactory" performance may meet the criteria imposed by one supervisor, but incur a reprimand from another, and the individual may experience this conflict of expectation as a source of stress.

The data from the large scale study of kibbutz members (Shirom, Eden, Siberwasser & Kellerman, 1973) indicate that there are differences between occupational groups. They found that occupations requiring greater physical exertion, e.g. agricultural workers, did not show this pronounced relationship between role ambiguity/role conflict and abnormal electrocardiographic readings. It is possible, therefore, that blue collar workers may suffer less from the interpersonal dynamics of the organisation, but more from the physical conditions of work.

(ii)   *Role ambiguity*

Role ambiguity results when the individual does not have adequate information about his work role and the behaviour that is expected. It also may be that the information is unclear, or confusing. The offshore oil and gas industry, like any other, has its own technical jargon (see glossary, Appendix I) which is unlike anything else experienced on construction sites, or in factories, and may thus add to possible confusion regarding instruction. This may also be compounded by the nature of the "cosmopolitan" workforce offshore and the possible communication difficulty because of language differences. Kahn, *et al.* (1964) found that men who suffered from role ambiguity experienced lower job satisfaction, high job-related tension, greater futility and lower self confidence. It is also related to indicators of physiological stress such as increased blood pressure and pulse rate (French & Caplan, 1970). In a representative national survey Margolis, Kroes & Quinn (1974) found that role ambiguity was related to stress indicators including depression, low motivation to work and intention to leave.

(iii)   *Responsibility*

Responsibility has been identified as a potential stressor associated with one's role in the organisation. A distinction is made between "responsibility for people" and "responsibility for things" (equipment, budgets etc.) and it is acknowledged that responsibility for people is significantly more likely to lead to C.H.D. than responsibility for things (Wardwell, Hyman & Bahnson, 1964; French & Caplan, 1970; Pincherle, 1970). For certain groups of offshore workers the aspect of "responsibility for people" may manifest in the form of "responsibility for the safety of others". For example, the crane driver knows that his mistake could kill the individual working on the deck below (Opbroek, 1983); the drilling crew must work as a co-ordinated team because lack of attention, or careless working, may cause injury to themselves or another member of the workcrew, and a mistake on the part of the petroleum engineer can result in a "blow-out" or explosion which can cause large scale injury or death, and actual total loss of the drilling rig itself. To date, investigation into this stressor of "responsibility for people" has focused on the element of supervision and management of others, and it is not known to what extent this sheer burden of the personal safety of others is a stress in the environment of the blue-collar workers offshore. However, lack of responsibility may also be a stressor for those groups of workers, and this is discussed in more detail in the section on job/work underload.

Relationships at work and interpersonal demands

The next major source of stress at work consists of interpersonal demands, and the nature of *relationships at work* with one's boss, peers and subordinates. Selye (1974) suggests that learning to live with other people is one of the most stressful aspects of life and Argyris (1964) and Cooper (1973) state that good relationships between members of a work group are a central factor in individual and organisational health. The issue is perhaps very important in the offshore drilling and production operation, where individuals work and live together in close proximity for long periods of time. It is not known to what extent this "constant company" factor may serve to accentuate or attenuate poor relationships at work. Poor relationships at work are defined as "low trust", "low levels of supportiveness" and "low interest in solving problems within the organisation". Mistrust is positively related to high role ambiguity, which leads to inadequate communication between individuals, and to psychological strain in the form of low job satisfaction and reduced well being (Kahn *et al.*, 1964; French & Caplan, 1973), but individuals forced to both live and work together may strive harder towards good working relationships "because" they must also live together.

Supportive social relationships with peers, supervisors and subordinates at work are less likely to create interpersonal pressures and will directly reduce levels of perceived job stress (Lazarus, 1966; McLean, 1979). It is suggested that social support such as group cohesion, interpersonal trust and liking for a supervisor, is associated with decreased levels of stress and better health (McLean, 1979) and, as work group cohesiveness increases, anxiety regarding work related matters decreases (Seashore, 1954). Generally social support makes people feel more positively about themselves and their work, and an empathetic supervisor may be a valuable prop to self esteem. McLean (1979) and Buck (1972) found that the inconsiderate behaviour of a supervisor appears to contribute significantly to feelings of job pressure.

Two further points should be made in this section on relationships at work and are related to the technical nature of the industry. Because of rapid change in technology, due to the need to cope with the challenging deep water environment of the North Sea, working relationships between boss and subordinate may be poor because the individual may feel that his boss has not kept up with, or adapted to, the new ways. It is also possible that the "new" employee is likely to be educated to a higher standard because of the need to produce ever higher qualifications in a keen jobs market. Lack of respect and confidence in a supervisor's ability is a poor foundation on which to build good working relationships. Also, supervisors with a technical or scientific background may regard relationships at work as low priority. Their orientation is towards "things", not "people" (Cooper & Marshall, 1978) and thus consideration of working relationships is viewed as mollycoddling, trivial, petty, time consuming and an impediment to doing the job well. Traditionally the offshore oil and gas extraction industry has the "American hire-and-fire mentality" (Moore & Wybrow, 1984), and "run-them-off" is the philosophy adopted at the slightest sign of a problem. But this attitude is slowly changing because it is recognised that more effort should be focused on selection of the "right" people to maintain a stable workforce, and that it makes sense to try and keep and develop good employees, especially in consideration of the investment made in training (financially and the time involved).

Interpersonal demands

These may also be potential sources of stress in the working environment. Quick & Quick (1984) identify five specific interpersonal stressors which come from the demands and pressures of social system relationships at work. They are status incongruence, social density, abrasive personalities, leadership style and group pressure, although it will be recognised that these factors may not be discussed completely in isolation from the issues reviewed under relationships at work, and thus some overlap will occur.

(i)   STATUS INCONGRUENCE

This may be perceived by the offshore worker because of either the job category he holds or by his nationality. The issue of the highly heterogeneous population offshore has already been discussed as a potential source of stress (Philbert *et al.*, 1975; Sunde, 1983; Hellesøy, 1985). Status incongruence may also occur as a result of offshore policy to employ workers from a contracting company. It is therefore possible that a situation can arise where two individuals may work side by side, doing exactly the same work, but in no respect equal as far as status is concerned (financial, job security nor promotion prospects). A "them-and-us" situation develops causing frustration and dissatisfaction; and the distress that subsequently arises may result in the reduced wellbeing of the individual and an increased vulnerability to accidents.

(ii)   SOCIAL DENSITY

Each individual has varying needs for interpersonal space and distance, and thus social density may be perceived as either too much or too little. Elliott (1985) describes the environment offshore as "a densely populated construction site, or factory, with specific risks" and, hence, this factor may be relevant to employees on drilling rigs and production platforms. In addition to long hours of shift working the individual cannot escape at the end of a day thus the constant company, often in crowded accommodation, may be a source of stress in the environment for some individuals, whereas others may regard it as a source of social stimulation and an alternative to loneliness onshore. However, evidence does suggest that crowding does lead to significant psychological stress, which contributes to both contagious and non-contagious illness (Cox, V. *et al.*, 1982); performance may suffer and job satisfaction deteriorates (Evans, 1969).

(iii)   ABRASIVE PERSONALITIES

These cause stress for other individuals because they ignore the interpersonal aspects of feelings and sensibilities of social interaction. The highly technical, achievement orientated, hard driving individual finds no time to consider working relationships and, as such, may be a source of interpersonal stress for others (Levinson, 1978).

(iv)   LEADERSHIP STYLE

The potential source of stress for individuals exposed to an authoritarian style of leadership is well documented (Lewin, Lippitt & White, 1939). There is a delicate balance between the positive effects of stimulating individuals towards growth and development and creating a negative environment of pressure and hostility. Tensions may be expressed either by an outwardly calm, passive, repressive attitude, which may physiologically manifest as elevated blood pressure, or there may be overt demonstrations of aggression and conflict. This may be healthier for the individual, but it may cause a stressful situation for the other workers.

Deterioration in working relationships between boss and subordinate may be destructive for the work group as a whole and lead to disrupted working relationships, reduced wellbeing and reduced safety consciousness.

(v)   GROUP PRESSURES

Both formal and informal groups in an organisation can put pressure on an individual, which is a source of stress in the working environment (Roethlisberger and Dickson, 1939) and, in the offshore industry, is perhaps more serious in that a "carry-over" effect may exist to extend any problems into the total working and living life of the individual while he is offshore. Although groups within the organisation can have a positive effect in that they offer social support and are a source of strength to the individual, it should be acknowledged that potential stress exists as a result of group pressure to conform to the norms of this unique work setting. Informal groups could develop offshore as a product of the heterogeneous population, and/or as a consequence of the individual's job category; the interpersonal demands of such groups or the conflict that may arise, could be sources of stress for the workers on drilling rigs and production platforms.

Career development

The fourth potential stressor includes factors of job insecurity, "over" and "under" promotion, thwarted ambition and social status incongruence. Although they are identified under the heading of "career development" it remains controversial as to how the concept of "career" may be defined, and if in fact it is the correct term to use when discussing blue-collar workers. However, for the purpose of this investigation into the oil and gas extraction industry, which includes the whole range of occupations from unskilled to highly technical and professional activities, the term will be applied to all levels of workers to refer to the job activities pursued over time, and which can involve several jobs and possibly occupations over the course of time (Hall, 1976). In this respect actual job change can also be stressful, but more relevant is perhaps the stress associated with job insecurity.

Job insecurity

This issue of job insecurity and fear of redundancy is a common feature of contemporary working life in these times of economic difficulties and high unemployment. The oil and gas extraction industry is also exposed to fluctuating world market prices, unstable political environments, and the gamble of discovery or dry holes in a new exploration area. Thus, the level of activity varies to meet these demands. Also, workers who decide to choose this way of life as a career must be prepared to be highly mobile if they are to stay in employment. For individuals employed as "contractors" the threat may be even greater as contracts are won or lost. They are aware that the employment is for a finite time, and that they must look for new employment every two years or so, hoping that a new contract is awarded somewhere to coincide with their current contract completion.

Over promotion; under promotion; thwarted ambition

Traditionally the offshore oil and gas industry has the reputation of promotion from within the ranks, and if ability and potential was demonstrated it was possible for example to promote from roustabout to be trained in one of the skilled and technical level occupations, perhaps as driller or petroleum engineer. "Tool pushers" commonly had a background of "starting-at-the-bottom". However, by necessity, the industry has become more complex and highly technical and there is also a keen and large labour market waiting to fill jobs, thus the qualifications and educational standards demanded have risen. Therefore, it is not known to what extent the lower level occupations now feel trapped in their job, without any hope of promotion, or perhaps the job is taken with the full knowledge that the individual will not be required to take on more responsibility than they want or feel able to cope with. Like all industry in today's economic climate, budget reviews are forced and cutbacks made usually include a reduction in personnel head count, as a cost reduction measure; and so perhaps even the highly skilled, higher level of occupations offshore may feel that promotion opportunities do not meet expectations. Brook (1973) describes case studies of individuals showing behavioural disorders ranging from minor psychological symptoms, psychosomatic complaints to more serious mental disorders, as a result of over or under promotion. Arthur & Gunderson (1965) found that promotion lag in a military environment was significantly related to psychiatric illness and job dissatisfaction.

Status incongruence

The issue of status incongruence is also relevant here, in that a potentially stressful situation may arise if the individual perceives a disparity between where he believes he should be in an organisation and the contrast of reality. This is in terms of both ability and social class.

Organisational structure and climate

The final potential source of organisational stress in these "external to the individual" categorisations is defined by Cooper & Marshall (1978) as simply "being in the organisation", and the threat to the individual's freedom, autonomy and identity that this poses.

One of the main issues here is that of worker participation. French & Caplan (1970) found that opportunity for participation in decision making produced significantly greater job satisfaction, higher feelings of self esteem and lower job related feelings of threat. In a national sample survey (Margolis, Kroes & Quinn, 1978) non-participation at work was a consistent and significant predictor of strain and job related stress. It was found to be related to health risk factors, including overall poor physical health, escapist drinking, depressed mood, low self esteem, low life satisfaction, low job satisfaction, low motivation to work, intention to leave job and absenteeism from work. Karasek (1979) generally supports these findings and suggests that restriction of opportunity for participation and autonomy increases depression, exhaustion, illness rates and pill consumption. Participation in decision making processes on the part of the individual may help to increase his "investment" in the organisation, create a sense of belonging and improve communication channels within the organisation. Neff (1968) suggests that it is the degree of perceived control that is the critical element of participation and involvement at work.

Regular safety meetings are compulsory for all offshore workers, and it is usually recognised as a chance to "speak-up" about any issue regarding conditions and work offshore. Whether the individual takes this opportunity and the degree to which it might make him feel that he has some level of control over his work and life offshore, is not yet known. Generally the "contractor personnel" do not have their own company supervisor offshore and answer directly to the operator in charge. Any grievance related to their own company must wait until they return to shore, and this could mean working and living with an unresolved problem for many days. Any time spent on office visits to discuss work related matters is therefore out of the individual's own free time. However, it is very likely that contractor personnel will have different problems related to organisational structure and climate than the operator personnel. Issues of company involvement and a sense of belonging may not be a source of stress because there are no expectations on the part of the "contracted" employee.

EXTRA-ORGANISATIONAL SOURCES OF STRESS

These sources of stress, external to the individual, include any element concerning the life of the person which interacts with his life inside the organisation. Personal life events will have an effect upon an individual's performance, effectiveness and adjustment at work (Bhagat, 1983) and must be taken into account when assessing sources of stress in the working environment. Livy and Vant (1979) indicate the importance of the problems of *family life* contributing as sources of stress for the individual offshore, in that it was cited by roustabouts and roughnecks as one of the main reasons for leaving offshore working. Issues concerning the family (Pahl & Pahl, 1971; Handy, 1978; Hall & Hall, 1980), life crisis (Dohrenwend & Dohrenwend, 1974), financial difficulties, conflicting personal beliefs with those of the company and the conflict of company with family demands, may put pressure on the individual at work.

But it should also be acknowledged that factors of personal life events may also mitigate the effects of organisational stressors, that is, *social support* acting as a buffer. House (1984) suggests that this is just one form of social support that is "emotional". Other forms include "instrumental", "informational" and "appraisal" support. The individual derives these forms of support from a variety of social relationships at work, home and in the community. For example, social support from a spouse may reduce the impact of job dissatisfaction on health by helping the individual to realise that the job is not all important in the total context of life; and dissatisfactions at work may be compensated for by satisfactions and accomplishments outside of work (McLean, 1979).

The *marriage/social relationships patterns* of the offshore worker is similar to that of the seafarer or other individuals who, by necessity, spend long periods of time working away from home. On average, he works six months of the year, usually on 1 or 2 week tours and with the equivalent free time at home. It may therefore be easier for the individuals to compartmentalise the different aspects of their lives and perhaps the successful offshore worker (in terms of mental well being, good physical health and accident free working) is the person who can leave any personal problems onshore while he is working, and not take his work problems home.

However, there are other potential stressors resulting from this way of life; these include factors such as coping with the *dependence* or *independence of one's spouse; assuming family roles* (husband, father etc.) and coping with the associated problems of regular absences from the home. Morrice (1985) describes the "intermittent husband syndrome" which results from the absence of husbands working offshore on an irregular/

regular basis and the stress of partings or reunions, which manifests in the reduced well being of the wives. He suggests that the "triad" of symptoms, "anxiety, depression and sexual difficulties", may be mirrored by the offshore husband. The study compares wives with offshore husbands with wives with onshore husbands doing similar work and supports the findings of Kreitman (1968) in that one partner's problems may contribute to the mental ill health of the other. However, because the offshore environment of a drilling rig or production platform is both quite unique and totally inaccessible to the spouse, it is difficult for a partner to relate to the life and to understand the working conditions and potential problems offshore.

Another factor within these marriage/social relationship patterns as a source of stress is the issue of *dual careers*. Because one of the partners is away from home for extended periods of time it does leave the other free to pursue a career, or an independent personal life, but if there are children to be considered then the partner left at home has full responsibility concerning them and must cope with any demands that arise, without the support of a partner. This might mean that the individual left at home is not free to fulfil career expectations. It may also be that the offshore worker is required to be *highly mobile* to stay in employment, and it might require relocating the whole family. This would provide added problems for the dual career couple. However, the trend appears to be towards leaving the spouse and family in a settled and safe environment, while the individual travels long distances to and from a location in some of the more inaccessible and hostile areas of the world (climatic and political). This usually entails the working of longer tours, for example, 28 days on, 28 days off. Other contracts might mean three or four months away from home at a time.

However, constant moving around is still a common factor to be considered as a potential stressor for the offshore worker. Families do not develop close ties with the local community (Immundo, 1974; Packard, 1971; Cooper, 1981 (2)), everything is treated as if it is temporary and the family remains indifferent to the local community amenities and organisation. In fact, it is common practice for the oilfield workers to set up their own communities and activities when they move en-masse to a new discovery area so, although contact may not be made with the locals, the same individuals can meet up at various locations worldwide and re-establish links of friendship. This may help the spouse to cope with *relocation* but the offshore worker is still denied the possibility of becoming involved in community life, clubs and many recreation activities (for example, sports teams and group activities) because of the lack of continuity in his life at home. Hence the offshore worker is still likely to retreat into his nuclear family when on leave (Pahl & Pahl, 1974).

Therefore, to understand psychosocial and occupational stressors for any particular group of employees, and the way stressors may manifest for the individual at work, it is vital to take an holistic approach in the course of the investigation. Organisational stress cannot be fully understood unless reference is made to those extra-organisational demands on the individual. However, to determine the ultimate individual costs of organisation and extra-organisation stress it is necessary to understand certain characteristics of the individual that may be "predisposers" to stress, or "modifiers" of the response to stress.

CHARACTERISTICS OF THE INDIVIDUAL

The contemporary, interactive view of stress is that situations are not inherently stressful. The behavioural, psychological or medical consequence of organisational stressors are the product of the particular situation, and the individual with his specific personality, behaviour pattern and life circumstances. Thus, the effect of potential stressors is not invariant between individuals, and "one man's meat is another man's poison" (Cassel, 1976). Different individuals will react differently to the same work environment, for example, one person enjoys working with lots of people around, while another finds it a source of stress or dissatisfaction, because of a lower need for interpersonal affiliation. Some individuals thrive on shift working (assessed in terms of mental and physical well being and accident free working), whereas another may develop hypertension or stomach ulcers. Occupational stressors therefore induce different types and degrees of stress in different workers. In this section these individual modifiers of the response to stress will be discussed.

Recent reviewers classify this "internal" contribution on the part of the individual in various ways. Innes (1981) describes "mediating factors" of a set of learned responses, which may be construed as fairly stable personality dispositions. These stable, individual differences in coping skills and the ability to learn them are recognised as making people more or less susceptible to stress. The issue is identified by Beehr & Newman (1978) as the "personal facet" which includes any characteristic of the human being that influences an individual's perception of stressful events, interpretation of events as stressful and/or the reaction to stress. In terms of job stress, researchers have investigated many factors, including "age", "ability", "personality", "needs" and physical condition. Schuler (1980) discusses the "internal" qualities of the individual under the categorisation of needs and values, abilities and experience and personality characteristics of the person. All are seen as important to the individual's subjective perception of organisational qualities.

The area of study to receive the most attention appears to be that of "personality characteristics". This will be discussed first, together with "behaviour pattern" factors, and the issues of "needs and values". The liberty of including these potential moderator variables under one heading is with an acknowledgement of the existence of the controversy of whether personality traits exist, or if they are innate or socially learned via social information processing (Mischel, 1976; Salancik & Pfeffer, 1978). Secondly, the individual qualities of ability and experience will be reviewed as a conditioning variable in the response to stressors in the environment. Thirdly, the issue of ethnicity will be briefly discussed in relation to the highly heterogeneous population working offshore: and, finally, the factors of "age" and physical condition will be considered; last but not least, to remind us that vulnerability at work is ever changing. Each life stage brings its own particular problems, and it must be remembered that response to stress is not static but a dynamic process.

Personality: behaviour patterns: needs/values

Many *personality* variables are implicated in the mediation of stress, and most research in this area has focused on personality differences between high and low stressed individuals. Typically this examines the relationship between various psychometric measures, for example, M.M.P.I. (Minnesota Multiphasic Personality Inventory) or the 16PF (Cattell's 16 Personality Factors Scale) and stress related diseases such as coronary heart disease (C.H.D.). Findings from several studies (reviewed by Jenkins, 1971a) indicate that patients with fatal C.H.D. tend to show greater neuroticism (particularly depression) in prospective M.M.P.I.'s than those who incur and survive coronary disease. Studies using the 16PF report findings of emotional instability (low scale C), high conformity and submissiveness (factor E) and desurgency/seriousness (factor F); high self sufficiency (factor Q2). Patients with C.H.D. or related illness are portrayed as emotionally unstable and introverted. However, most of the studies were retrospective and thus the characteristics reported may be a reaction to C.H.D. and not a precursor of it.

Other dimensions of personality which are likely to interact with stress include introversion/extraversion (Brebner & Cooper, 1978). The extrovert is viewed as "geared to respond" and will attempt a response when given an opportunity whereas the introvert may inhibit a response and seek more information. This finding may be related to the work of

Zuckerman (1974) in that "sensation-seeking" individuals will be less severely affected by life events than the low scoring individual at the other pole of the dimension with a tendency to "dampen down" situations. An important point to consider here is the "self-selection" of individuals into a particular occupation. It is therefore necessary to recognise that individuals with certain characteristics may be attracted to a certain job. Thus it follows that offshore workers could be sensation seeking extroverts who are attracted to this unique relatively new working situation of the drilling rig or production platform. Workers who are compatible will survive best, or longer than others, who will move away or function poorly (McMichael, 1978).

The investigation by Kahn *et al.* (1964) into role conflict and role ambiguity also included personality measures from a full range of occupations (first-time supervisors and upwards). Response to role conflict was found to be mediated or "conditioned" by the personality of the individual. For example, anxiety prone people experienced the conflict as more intense; introverts suffered more tensions and reported more deterioration in interpersonal relations; "flexibles" (versus "rigids") were more open to influence from other people and were more likely to become overloaded, but "rigids" were more susceptible to rush jobs from above. These findings are supported by Brief (1981), introversion, extraversion, flexibility, rigidity and dogmatism; Chan (1977), anxiety; and Ivancevich & Matteson (1980), tolerance for ambiguity; and were all found to be personality factors which are associated with individual response to organisational stress.

Self esteem also appears to be an important individual trait in the workplace. Mueller (1965) suggests that individuals with self reported low esteem were also more likely to perceive greater work overload. House (1972) and Kasl & Cobb (1970) believe that self esteem acts as a buffer against adverse stress reaction, and C.H.D. risk factors rise as self esteem declines.

Another characteristic of the individual which may be an important moderator of stressors in the environment is *"locus of control"* (Rotter, 1966). This is based on a Social Learning Theory, "Interactionist" view of the person, in that the individual learns from the environment through "modelling" and past experience. Reinforcement of a certain behaviour has an effect on expectancy and so eventually expectancy leads to behaviour. "Locus of control" refers to the extent to which the individual perceives that he has control over a given situation. The person who is characterised as an "internal" believes that his decisions and actions will influence what happens to him. The belief that he plays a role in determining the events that impinge upon him is viewed as a factor in the expectation of coping with a stressful situation, thus he suffers less threat and fewer adverse reactions than the externally orientated individuals who tend to believe in luck or fate, and that they do not have any control over their environment. However, "internals" will experience more anxiety in a situation in which they perceive that they have no control.

The issue of perceived level of control in the work situation has been extensively studied in relationship to noise as a stressor in the environment. The work of Glass & Singer (1972) highlights the importance of the individual's perception of noise in a given situation. The extent to which the worker believes he is in control of the noise and the ability to predict or govern its onset, appears to be crucial in mediating disruption of both mood and performance (Graeven, 1975; Jones, D., 1983). The importance of categorisation of individuals as "internals" or "externals" may therefore be relevant in that it is acknowledged that subjective experience of noise may be more crucial than the objective measurement of environmental noise. The noise factor of offshore working is a recognised potential hazard in the environment that not only affects the individual while he is working, but is also a potential source of annoyance and irritation during free time, in the living and leisure areas. It may therefore be that internally orientated individuals suffer more from noise in the environment because it is a situation over which they have no control.

However, Lefcourt (1970) warns that locus of control is not a trait nor a typology and people are not totally internals or externals. Also, locus of control should not be expected to account for a lion's share of the variance in a situation; it is only one singular expectancy construct, and other interacting variables must be taken into account.

This "subjective experience" factor is the focal point for assessing a job stress measure known as "Person-Environment-Fit" (P-E Fit) (Van Harrison, 1975; French, 1979; and Caplan, 1983). P-E Fit is assessed by asking subjects to indicate "desired" and "actual" levels of work related factors, such as role ambiguity, workload and responsibility, and looking at the differences between the scores. Misfit is defined by either demand exceeding a person's capability/capacity or if capability/capacity exceeds demand. Resultant stress manifests in problems such as depression, job dissatisfaction and anxiety. However, studies only show moderate correlations between misfit and various stress outcomes (Caplan, 1983). This poor predictive power may be overcome by the recently presented elaboration of the original model.

However, the issue to receive the most attention from researchers is the *behaviour pattern* identified as the coronary prone *"Type-A"* person. The original characteristics of the coronary patient were described by Dunbar (1943) as "compulsively striving, with an urge to get to the top through hard work, self discipline and mastery of others". Yet the Type A/Type B behaviour pattern is attributed to Friedman & Rosenman (Friedman, 1969; Rosenman, Friedman & Strauss, 1964, 1966), based on their large scale, national sample, the "Western Collaborative Group Study" (W.C.G.S.). The most frequent cause of death in western society today is from coronary heart disease and the related circulatory disorders; as such, the Type A versus Type B differentiation and its association with an increased risk of heart disease have received a great deal of attention from researchers on a world-wide basis. W.C.G.S. is a prospective study of 35,000 men which began in 1959 and has continued over the years to produce data of an epidemiological, pathological and biochemical nature, relating aggressive emotion with a high risk of getting C.H.D. (Carruthers, 1980). The study also confirms the importance of such factors as family history of C.H.D., elevated systolic and diastolic blood pressures, cigarette smoking, level of education and higher serum levels of cholesterol, beta lipoproteins and neutral fat.

The original study began by classifying individuals as "A" or "B" types on the basis of structured interviews; none had any prior record of heart disease. Results of follow-up investigations at regular intervals have confirmed the Type A behaviour pattern as a precursor of C.H.D., independent of the standard risk factors (Rosenman *et al.*, 1964, 1975). Those judged to be Type A at the offset of the study had twice the rate of clinical coronary diseases, were five times as likely to have a second myocardial infarction and had twice the rate of fatal heart attacks experienced by the Type B subjects at follow-up (8.5 year point). Type A individuals strive more diligently towards achievement, are more perfectionist, tense, impatient, unable to relax, put more effort into the job/or profession, are more active and energetic than the corresponding "B Type" individuals. (Chesney & Rosenman, 1980, provide a review of the laboratory studies on Type A behaviour and reactivity.) Type A is characterised by extremes of competitiveness, aggressiveness, feelings of time pressure and the challenge of responsibility, to the extent that commitment to work results in the relative neglect of other aspects of their lives (Jenkins, 1971b). Research continually shows that Type A behaviour may be reliably rated as a deeply ingrained, enduring trait (Jenkins, 1976) and Beehr & Newman (1978) discuss this issue of Type A/B in terms of being a personality or a behaviour. However, McMichael (1978) maintains that it is not a trait, but a style of behaviour and a habitual response to circumstance. It is thus a behaviour predisposition which may be a potent conditioning variable. The assumption here is that behaviour can be changed, and although there is no doubt that this deleterious pattern exists, the extent to which an individual can change, to prevent heart disease, is not fully understood. It should also be remembered that neat categorisations are dangerous in that they seem oversimplified, and are thus equally simple to rectify. They also represent extremes of behaviour, whereas most individuals are somewhere in the middle along a continuum of the Type A/Type B behaviour pattern. Again the issue of "self-selection" into jobs that entail a greater exposure to stimulation or stressors needs to be considered, in that persons with a particular personality and behaviour characteristics might seek out a certain type of work environment. This idea is supported by the findings of Caplan *et al.* (1975). It may also be that Type A individuals are more prone to perceive stress in an exaggerated fashion (Caplan, 1971). It would however appear that these individuals experience more stress at work and more C.H.D., with the latter apparently due partially to the former (House, 1974b).

Implicit in this discussion is that personality, viewed as either stable, enduring traits or as learned behaviour results in a predisposition to respond in a certain way, and is therefore an important moderator variable in the response to a stressor in the environment. The presence or absence of a trait or behaviour pattern increases or decreases the likelihood that a particular event or condition will be perceived as stressful (Quick & Quick, 1984). This also applies to the *needs and values* of an individual which are viewed as defining the desires of the individual, in helping to determine the perception of opportunity, constraint and demands of the environment, and the relative importance of the outcomes (Schuler, 1980). Needs and values identified as mediators in the response to organisational stressors include "achievement" (Seashore, 1972; McClelland, 1965; Herzberg, 1978); "self control, certainty and predictability" (Zaleznik *et al.*, 1977); "feedback" (Corson, 1971); "fairness and justice" (Adams, 1965); "interpersonal recognition and acceptance" (Volicer, 1974); "ethical conduct" (Kahn *et al.*, 1964); "responsibility and meaningfulness and purpose" (Hackman & Oldham, 1975); "personal space and ownership" (Sundstrom, 1977); "stimulation" (Levi, 1967) and "intrinsic satisfaction" (Harrison, 1975). Knowing an individual's needs and values, whether innate or learned, is necessary in understanding whether the individual will experience stress from his perception of the working environment.

Abilities and experience

Research on "ability" and "experience" as moderators of the response to organisational stress is scarce but they are viewed as potentially important in that they influence perception of opportunity, demand and constraint and, consequently, the choice of strategy to deal with a stressor (Schuler, 1980).

The factor of "ability" is incorporated in the research on role/work overload (Kahn *et al.*, 1964) in that quantitative overload (French & Caplan, 1973) may be interpreted in terms of the ability of the employee, as well as the time available to do the job (Beehr & Newman, 1978) and a worker with more ability can accomplish more work in less time than an employee with less ability for the job. In this light Sales (1970) has shown that objective quantitative overload is negatively related to self esteem, and positively to tension and heart rate and French & Caplan (1973) support this finding, but with reported "subjective" measures of work overload. The existence of qualitative work overload (described by French & Caplan, 1973) also relates to this moderator variable of "ability" in that some employees could not complete the work successfully, regardless of the time allowed, because they do not have the skill required to do the job and would thus experience qualitative work overload as stressful.

McGrath (1970) suggests that "experience" should also be considered as a moderator of the response to stressors in the work environment. This is in terms of "familiarity" with the situation. Past exposure, practice and training to deal with a situation can operate to effect the level of subjectively experienced stress, by reducing uncertainty, and thus modify the reaction to that stressor. This may perhaps explain why the method of "role-play" is more successful in attitude/behaviour change in training situations (for example educational and safety campaigns) than lectures, posters or discussions alone (Janis & Mann, 1965).

Ethnicity

Membership of a particular racial or minority group can have an effect on an individual's response to a stressor in the environment, in addition to being a source of stress itself (that is belonging to a particular ethnic group, or a minority group). Expectations and aspirations of the individual will affect the perception of opportunity, constraint and demand, and may be more acute for members of a minority group where different cultural and social factors may magnify the source of stress, for example, status incongruence in interpersonal relationships at work.

Age and physical condition

Age is an important consideration as a moderator variable of stress in the environment in that each stage of life has its own particular vulnerability and coping mechanism (McLean, 1979). Thus an examination of potential stressors, for example, career development, over and under promotion and thwarted ambition, can only be fully understood in relation to the stage of life of the individual concerned. As Levinson (1978) states, there are seasons of a man's life which when documented will point to likely periods of stress and why they occur. In a study of middle-aged construction workers Theorell (1976) found the measure of "discord" among employees to be much higher in the 41-56 age group than the 56-65 age group and may therefore suggest that age may perform a moderator role in job stress, linked perhaps to factors such as expectation and aspiration. The impact of stress may be influenced by an individual's age in two ways. First, age may in part determine whether a situation is perceived as a stressor and, secondly, the individual biological condition may determine how the stress response manifests. Thus age is linked with factors such as "experience" and "physical condition" as mediators in the response to stressors at work: and so, finally, the issue of *physical condition* is viewed as a logical predictor of illness. Hennigan & Wortham (1979) have demonstrated that individuals in good physical condition, and who are not cigarette smokers, are able to maintain a low heart rate during the normal stress of the workday, whereas stress is more likely to increase the heart rate of others less physically fit.

Individual qualities or characteristics are thus used to explain the level of stress an individual might experience. Many areas of this "personal facet" still require investigation and much of the research to date is correlational and therefore leaves questions of causation unanswered (Beehr & Newman, 1978). However, the need to consider the individual contribution is vital in the understanding of the psychological, physical and behavioural response to stressors in the organisational environment.

6 Methodology

A review of the literature, Section 3, indicates that no attempt has been made to identify psychosocial and occupational sources of stress among offshore workers in the Dutch and U.K. sectors of the North Sea. Investigation into the psychosocial aspects of work offshore on the Norwegian Continental Shelf (Hellesøy, 1985; Sunde, 1983) is in progress, but to date only descriptive and anecdotal accounts exist, generally about the lives and working and living conditions of the personnel employed on drilling rigs and production platforms offshore. It was therefore the aim of this study to identify the sources of psychosocial and occupational stress among this unique occupational group involved in oil and gas extraction from subsea locations.

RESEARCH DESIGN

Phase I — interviews

This involved conducting semi-structured interviews with a representative, random sample of personnel working offshore on both drilling and production installations in the U.K. and Dutch sectors of the North Sea. The sample included a cross section of the various occupations employed by the company, and incorporated factors of skill level, working pattern (that is, both number of days offshore, e.g. 7 or 14, and type of shift, e.g. days only, day and night working etc.), and distance travelled to the check-in point (that is, short distance of, for example, 2 hours travel time; medium distance, approximately 7-8 hours travel time; and long distance, requiring an overnight stay to meet an early morning crew change).

Employees were introduced in advance to the project by way of company correspondence and newsletter. The content of this was agreed by way of joint discussion. Individuals were selected prior to the interview date on a random basis from passenger flight lists issued for crew change operations, and invited to take part in the study. Only two individuals did not appear at the agreed time of interview. The interviews were carried out over a two week period of time on the day of crew change. The Dutch sector interviews were conducted actually at the heliport terminals (two locations), and the U.K. sector interviews were held in an hotel adjacent to the heliport. Some individuals were interviewed on return from a tour of duty, and others just prior to departure. Interviews lasted 40 to 50 minutes. A total of 31 interviews were completed, this being a 5% sample of the then total workforce. Nine interviews were recorded on tape with the agreement of the interviewees. The interviewer's previous link with the industry was made known, to establish some sort of rapport and put the individuals at ease, but also as an attempt to assure that a certain level of knowledge and understanding could be expected. All individuals were reminded that complete confidentiality was guaranteed, and that the information from the interviews would be used to generate a questionnaire which eventually would be sent to all company employees. A prepared interview schedule, based on the model "sources of stress" proposed by Cooper & Marshall (1978), was used in order to make quick notes as unobtrusively as possible (Appendix II), and to remind the interviewer of the points that should be covered.

(1)   Factors intrinsic to the job.
(2)   Role in the organisation.
(3)   Career development.
(4)   Relationships at work.
(5)   Organisation and climate.
(6)   Home/work interface.

No attempt was made to discuss these issues in any particular order, although the interviews were all started in the same way, in that interviewees were encouraged to start talking by asking, "Tell me about your job". If necessary, prompts were given to keep the individual talking and to ensure that all the various aspects related to life and working conditions were included. Because of the relatively short interview period it was often necessary to ask direct questions in some cases, for example, concerning "career development", "Tell me about your plans for the future"; and concerning responsibility, "What are the repercussions of making a mistake?". Each interview was concluded with the same two questions, "What is the best and worst thing about life and work at the moment?"; and, "Are there any changes you would make if given the opportunity?".

Phase II — designing the Questionnaire

Section B: sources of stress

After completing all the interviews, transcripts of the audio-tapes were made. From these and the prepared interview schedules, items were identified as potential sources of stress among these offshore workers, but also keeping in mind that one man's meat is another man's poison (Cassel, 1976) and positive issues raised by some individuals may be negative factors for others. Care was taken to present simple, short statements in the final list of factors. These were scrutinised by independent parties, both related and non-related to the industry for criticism and evaluation of understanding, and subsequent adjustments were made accordingly. The final questionnaire contained 74 potential sources of stress (Appendix III, Section B). Two questions contained multiple responses (Nos. 23 and 26) concerning ergonomic factors of noise, heat, cold and vibration, thus making a total of 80 responses. A five point Likert type scale was used with a low score indicating "no stress" and the high score indicating "high stress". The option to indicate "not applicable" (NA) was also included, for example, a factor relating to one's wife could be scored "NA" by the single respondents. A short explanation of the meaning attached to this part of the questionnaire, and the points of the scale, was included. A definition of stress was also given. This acknowledged that the subjective experience of stress is open to many different interpretations. Hence the author was guided by the terms expressed during the interviews and previous studies of this kind. Although the individuals were fully aware of the objectives of the investigation, they used many different terms. For example, "I worry about the inexperienced guys who are put out here, it's my neck as well as theirs". Thus the definition used was, "The word 'stress' should be interpreted in a wide sense, that is, worry, tension, anxiety, anger or perhaps just mild irritation".

The questionnaire also included a request for the following information.

Section A	Demographic data
Section B	Work environment stressors (already discussed)
Section C	Accident and health behaviours
Section D	Job satisfaction
Section E	Crown Crisp Experiential Index
Section F	Type "A" Coronary Prone Behaviour Index
Section G	Personality factor; "Locus of control"
Section H	Any further comments

Each section will be briefly reviewed in turn.

Section A: demographic data

This included the request for standard biographical data, information concerning the individual's present offshore work and his occupation prior to working in the offshore drilling and production environment. The decision to include this last item was the result of information generated from the interviews in part one of the study. It was observed that some individuals were doing exactly the same job offshore as they had onshore, whereas others had a totally unrelated occupation. There also appeared to be a high proportion of individuals with a seafaring background, and some of them indicated that this factor may be an important aspect in the process of coping with life on offshore drilling rigs and production platforms. Knowledge of an individual's background may therefore be important to the understanding of reported sources of stress at work.

The final items covered, in Section A of the questionnaire (Appendix II), included:

(1) Job title
(2) Skill level
(3) Type of installation: production or drilling. Experience of both types of installation.
(4) Name of installation
(5) Number of people on the installation
(6) Details of work tour; the number of days and the shift pattern
(7) Number of years in the industry
(8) Number of years with the present company
(9) Job held prior to offshore working
(10) Age
(11) Marital status
(12) Number and age of children
(13) Education
(14) Technical qualifications. (Interview data suggested that many individuals did not have education qualifications identifiable under the standard questionnaire format, but had left formal schooling at 15/16 to serve an apprenticeship for their particular trade.)
(15) Supervision of others

Section C: accident and health behaviours

(i) ACCIDENTS

A reduction in the frequency of accidents offshore, resulting in injuries, fatalities and damage to plant and equipment is the priority of all companies involved in the oil and gas extractive industry. Frequent and severe accidents are a recognised symptom of stress at work (Cooper, 1981). Statistics consistently show that more accidents, leading to death and serious injury, occur on drilling operations rather than production platforms (Tables 2.5 and 2.6). Therefore, a request for details of accidents at work was included in the questionnaire (Appendix III). This includes a brief description of the incident, the time of day it happened and the day of the particular "hitch" (that is the tour of duty, for example, "2 of 7" indicates that the accident happened on the second day of a seven day period of time offshore. The term is a common expression within the industry.) Although not statistically proven, information presented by the International Labour Office (1978) suggests that most accidents occur during the first one or two days or the last one or two days spent offshore, irrespective of the length of "hitch". An attempt was thus made to see to what extent this investigation supports this idea. "Lost time" information was also requested as an indication of the seriousness of the incident.

(ii) ILLNESS

Information regarding time lost due to personal or family illness was also sought (Appendix III), in order to ascertain the type of illness specified with the level of seriousness expressed in "working time lost", in order to compare the health behaviours of drilling rig and production platform crews. An acknowledgement of the importance of an interactive effect between the home and work interface makes it vital to identify both personal and family illness. Although some problems exist with replication of the study, Verhaegen, *et al.*, (1976) demonstrated that individuals who were responsible for an accident differed by their "heavier psychological burden" from the people who were "victims" of accidents. "Heavier psychological burden" was defined in terms of worries about children and marital partners etc. This information will be used to see if any relationship exists between the incidence of reported illness, the report of sources of stress in the environment, increased vulnerability to accidents, and/or the measure of mental health.

(iii) ALCOHOL CONSUMPTION LEVEL

Alcohol consumption is a recognised serious reaction to psychosocial and occupational stress. Many studies suggest that one's occupation may be an influential factor in determining drinking habits and consequently alcohol related problems (Plant, 1979a; Ojesjo, 1980). Margolis *et al.* (1974), and Hurrell & Kroes (1975) found that those experiencing high job stress drank more than those in occupations experiencing less job stress. The offshore environment is unusual in that alcohol is banned offshore and so the individual must go completely without alcohol during the time spent on the rig or platform. The extent to which this rule is adhered to is not known, as Robert Burke the editor of *"Offshore"* (August 1985) suggests, "One aspect of safety not discussed in polite places is the use and abuse of drugs and alcohol on a rig". He believes that it has become a most serious problem for rig operators and is one that is destined to draw more attention before safety figures can improve. However, at this stage this investigation only focused on questions concerning the drinking habits of individuals while they were on shore leave, in order to examine any possible relationship between reported sources of stress and the amount of alcohol regularly consumed.

(iv) CIGARETTE SMOKING

Cigarette smoking is related to the incidence of coronary heart disease (Selye, 1976) and is also associated with neuroticism and anxiety (McCrae *et al.*, 1978). The relationship between cigarette smoking and Type A coronary prone behaviour (see Section E) is well documented. Caplan *et al.* (1975) found that Type As are less likely to give up smoking than B Types, and Howard *et al.* (1976) demonstrated that managers with extreme type A behaviour had a higher percentage of cigarette smokers than the Type B behaviour pattern individuals. Over time these behaviours will lead to an increase in the association between smoking and the risk of coronary heart disease (Cooper, 1981). Comments arising from the interviews in Phase I of the study suggest that some individuals adopt different patterns in their cigarette smoking behaviours offshore and when onshore during leave time. Therefore a question was included to examine this behaviour (Appendix III, question 12). The restricted opportunity to smoke during the 12 hour working day may be an additional source of stress for an individual who habitually smokes many more cigarettes a day when he is at home. It should also be noted that offshore personnel have access to duty free supplies of tobacco while they are on the rig or platform and so, continually increasing high cost is not motivation or incentive to give up the habit.

(v)   HEALTH BEHAVIOURS

The last two questions in this section (questions 13 and 14) were included to examine the measures used by individuals to relax, and to see if exercise was a regular part of their lives. The question, "How often do you use the following measures to relax?" was presented in a Likert format, and allowed a response of "never, rarely, sometimes, often or always". In addition to the repetition of smoking and drinking behaviours the list included the taking of sleeping pills, use of tranquilisers, use of stimulants such as coffee and coke, and eating junk food. The final three items were behavioural methods of relaxation that is taking exercise, talking to someone you know, and the use of humour. An opportunity to add "other" items to the list was also included. Individuals were also asked if they took regular exercise, with a request for detail of the type of activity and frequency. The importance of regular physical exercise is well documented. Hammond (1964) showed a strong correlation between exercise and longevity; Lynch *et al.* (1973) demonstrated that regular exercise had both physiological and psychological benefit, that is, a reduction in measures of anxiety, depression and hostility. Clinically depressed patients were observed to improve with the introduction of running therapy. The physiological benefits of regular exercise have been found to decrease resting heart rate and blood pressure (Fentem & Bassey, 1978; Yvarvote *et al.*, 1974). Although it has not been proven whether a programme of regular aerobic exercise later in life will have an effect on cardiovascular disease and heart attack prevention (Quick & Quick, 1984), the effect of reducing blood pressure would appear to be beneficial for Type A behaviour pattern individuals observed to have higher blood pressure and cholesterol levels than Type B individuals (Rosenman *et al.*, 1964, 1966). The various health behaviour measures may therefore be examined in relationship to reported sources of stress, measure of mental health and the reported degree of job satisfaction.

Section D: the job satisfaction scale

In order to compare levels of job satisfaction among offshore workers with blue collar workers onshore in the United Kingdom, and to compare reported degrees of job satisfaction between drilling rig and production platform personnel, Warr, Cook & Wall's "Job Satisfaction Scale" was selected (Appendix III, Section D). The scale was developed on a stratified sample of blue collar workers in the United Kingdom, and good reliability is reported (Alpha co-efficients of .85 and .88 reported for samples of 200 and 390 respectively). The Job Satisfaction Scale consists of a 16 item, seven point response measure, with "one" being the most negative response. Although a global measure was required at this stage of analysis, the measure also yields five subscales of specific aspects of satisfaction (intrinsic job satisfaction; extrinsic job satisfaction; job itself intrinsic satisfaction; working conditions extrinsic satisfaction and employee relations satisfaction) and these may be utilised in further analysis.

Section E: the Crown Crisp Experiential Index

The Crown Crisp Experiential Index (C.C.E.I.), formerly known as the Middlesex Questionnaire (Crown & Crisp, 1966), was chosen to measure the mental health of offshore workers by means of a postal survey (Appendix III, Section E). C.C.E.I. consists of 48 questions designed rapidly to quantify common symptoms and traits which are relevant to the conventional categories of psycho-neurotic illness and personality disorders (Crown & Crisp, 1979). The objective is to obtain an approximation to the diagnostic information that would be gained from a formal clinical psychiatric examination. It is proven to be a reliable, valid, objective test for which normative data is available. A total score is obtained to provide a measure of general emotionality or "neuroticism", together with a profile of six subscales: free floating anxiety (F.F.A.); phobic anxiety (PHO); obsessionality (OBS); somatic concomitants of anxiety (Som.); depression (Dep.); and hysterical personality (HYS). Two points need to be mentioned at this time; first, the validity of the hysteria subscale (HYS) is questionable. It correlates highly with the "E" (extraversion) scale of the Eysenck Personality Inventory (Young *et al.*, 1971), and may be a better measure of sociability and extraversion (Crisp, Gaynor-Jones & Slater, 1978); and reservation also exists about the phobic anxiety measure (PHO) in that phobias are usually specific and the scale only includes common phobias such as fear of heights, illness, crowds and open spaces etc.

Section F: Type A Coronary Prone Behaviour Index

Type A behaviour pattern is a well documented coronary heart disease (C.H.D.) risk factor (Rosenman *et al.*, 1964; Haynes *et al.*, 1978a, 1978b, 1980). It was therefore decided to examine the prevalence of the Type A behaviour pattern in this offshore environment, and to see if any differences exist between workers on drilling rig and production platform installations. Caplan *et al.* (1975), Sales (1969) and McMichael (1978) suggest that different group experiences of job stress may in part reflect differences in the type of person within the job and thereby support the notion of "self selection" into jobs. This also includes selection by employers and changes in personality traits as a result of socialisation by the job; in fact Frankenhauser (1970) suggests that occupational stressors can in fact encourage Type A behaviour patterns.

The focus of most study of Type A Coronary-Prone Behaviour Pattern and risk of C.H.D. is on white collar and professional workers. The original study, "W.C.G.S.", included only 10% blue collar workers, and many other investigations are restricted to middle and upper levels of managerial and technical-scientific work (Rosenman *et al.*, 1964). Haynes *et al.* (1981) suggest that Type A behaviour was a significant risk factor for C.H.D. over a ten year period among men employed in white collar jobs, but not significantly so for their blue collar worker sample described as "clerical and kindred, manual protective and service workers". However, Kasl (1978) suggests that we do not know if Type A behaviour is a risk factor for blue collar workers, or how it varies as a risk factor across different occupational and work settings. Thus, the opportunity to examine this group of blue collar workers in terms of Type A/Type B Coronary Prone Behaviour was taken by including the short questionnaire known as "The Framingham type A behaviour scale" (Hayes *et al.*, 1978) (Appendix III, Section F). This is designed to measure coronary prone behaviour identified as a sense of time urgency and competitiveness, and was developed from the Framingham Heart Study, which included both women and men working in a variety of occupational settings. The 10 item questionnaire gives an overall raw score of Type A behaviour (with a cut-off point at 0.399 for males). It will therefore be possible to compare the reported sources of stress between individuals identified as either Type As or Type Bs, and examine any differences in mental health and job satisfaction measures.

Section G: personality factor locus of control

The perception of control is viewed as a potential moderator of stress (Lefcourt, 1973). The characteristic is concerned with the degree to which individuals perceive that they have control over events. Information emerging from the interviews in Phase I of the study appeared to suggest that individuals working offshore generally feel that they do not have any control over what is going on around them. Thus, the decision was made to examine the prevalence of "internals" and "externals" in the offshore environment and to compare any differences in reported sources of stress. Internally orientated individuals believe that their decisions and their actions will influence what happens to them, and externally orientated individuals tend to believe that rewards and positive reinforcements are beyond their control; they are believers in luck and fate (Quick & Quick, 1984). Investigations in field settings generally have taken the form of examining particular stressors for their impact on emotional disturbance and illness, and it would appear that internals, perceiving themselves to have greater control, tend to be less threatened by the stressful situations, and thus experience fewer adverse reactions. Internals therefore seem better equipped to survive their ordeals (Lefcourt, 1983). However, they may experience more anxiety in situations where they have little or no control.

In the offshore environment noise is an acknowledged hazard and potential source of stress which would not be under the control of the internally orientated individual and thus he might be expected to suffer more adverse effects. It may therefore also be possible that again the "self-selection" of individuals into occupations is in operation, with a high proportion of "externally orientated" individuals working on the drilling rig installations. There is also some support for the suggestion that individuals with an external locus of control may be prone to more frequent or heavier drinking, and drinking as a means of coping with psychological distress to a greater extent than those with a more internal locus of control (Donovan & O'Leary, 1983; Cox, 1979).

The I-E Scale (Rotter, 1966) was used to measure locus of control (Appendix III). This is a twenty-nine item, forced-choice measure of the tendency towards an internal or external locus of control. It includes six filler items intended to disguise the aims of the test, and takes approximately fifteen minutes to complete. The measure has demonstrated internal consistency, test-retest reliability, and discriminant validity, although it has been criticised for its relation to social desirability (Joe, 1971).

Section H

This was included as an opportunity for each individual to add any additional information that might be relevant to the study; for example, about personal experiences, or techniques/personal characteristics found to be personally useful for coping with this working and living environment (Appendix II).

Designing the questionnaire – conclusion

The questionnaire was completed by the addition of a page of general instructions (Appendix III) including general comments on how to answer, how to correct any changes required, and points that were necessary to accompany a postal survey. A reminder about the objectives of the study was also added, and a further assurance of confidentiality.

The title page of the final booklet took the form of an introductory letter produced on university headed paper. This included the purpose of the study, and an acknowledgement that the issue of the questionnaire had the full support of the company involved. The background to the development of the questionnaire (Phase I) was briefly explained, and instructions for its return were given. All personnel were reminded that the results of the project would be presented to the company and made available to anyone interested. The company newsletter would continue to keep them informed of the progress of the study.

Phase III — questionnaire distribution and return

The final questionnaire was printed by the company at their head office, together with an addressed envelope for return directly to the University of Manchester on completion. It was decided by the company that a full English-Dutch translation would not be necessary for Dutch employees in general, but they were all provided with a translation of comparable educational levels for the Netherlands. A total of 742 questionnaires and pre-addressed, stamped envelopes were despatched by mail directly to the homes of the employees during the first week of August. This constitutes all offshore personnel employed by the company in the U.K. and Dutch sectors of the North Sea. Names and addresses were generated from a computer based mailing list. A cut-off time for the return of questionnaires was set, allowing an eight week return period and, at the end of the specified time, a total of 218 had been received in Manchester; this constitutes an almost 30% rate of return, 103 from the U.K. sector (34% return) and 115 from the Dutch sector (26% return). Two questionnaires were returned uncompleted by the addressees, with notes advising that English language ability was not adequate to enable completion of the form. Others had insufficient data completed to justify including them in the sample. Therefore, a total of 194 completed questionnaires were usable to carry out the study on sources of psychosocial and occupational stress in the offshore oil and gas extractive industries.

Phase IV — data preparation

The returned questionnaires were checked, and the standard questionnaires were scored, that is:

Section D   Job Satisfaction Scale
Section E   Crown-Crisp Experiential Index
Section F   The Framingham Type "A" Behaviour Scale
Section G   I-E Scale (Locus of control)

These scores, and the remainder of the data, were transferred to the data-coding section on the right-hand side of each page of the questionnaire booklet (Appendix III) ready for data input by the University of Manchester Regional Computing Centre. Scoring and questionnaire coding checks were carried out by an independent party. A file, using the Statistical Package for the Social Sciences (Nie, Hull, Jenkins *et al.*, 1975), was created.

RESEARCH OBJECTIVES

As stated, the aim of the study was to identify sources of psychosocial and occupational stress among offshore workers on drilling rigs and production platforms in the North Sea oil and gas extraction industry.

However, from information generated in Phase I of the study, the interviews, it became apparent that perhaps it would be necessary to observe these individuals in terms of two distinct groups, that is, those employed on drilling rig operations and those employed on production platform installations, and that sources of stress at work may be different within these two distinct occupational environments. Several quotes emerge to support this suggestion. For example:

Production platform workers

"I've experienced two blow-outs (on drilling rigs). ... I wouldn't want to go through that again."

"It's more stable than the drilling job ... when the job finishes the rig may move away ... then perhaps no other job is going ... the production is more stable."

"My wife, she prefers me on the production ... it's more safe ... me, I prefer the drilling ... more busy ... more activity."

Drilling rig workers

A derrickman: "No! I wouldn't want to work on a production platform ... it's too hum-drum."

A crane operator: "The work is much harder ... it's twelve hours of hard work most of the time."

Individuals with experience of both

"The whole life there [drilling rig] is different ... they are working at night ... the damage is plenty, so you are never sure you can sleep at night" (a day worker on breakdown call-out at night).

And, during a discussion about noise on a production platform, "There is no problem here ... but it's different on the drilling."

It was also realised that differences may exist between workers on production platforms in the Dutch and U.K. sectors. One striking difference is the comparative size of the installations; that is, small clusters of platforms in the Dutch sector (which is known as the Southern Sector of the North Sea) with relatively few personnel on board, for example, 40–50 workers, and some much less, whereas the production installations in the North Sea that are serviced out of Scotland commonly have two to three hundred workers offshore at any given time. The final analysis should therefore examine any differences in terms of this Southern/Northern North Sea sectors split.

The final justification for examining this offshore population as distinct categories of "drilling" and "production" workers is based on the accident statistics available. On the Dutch sector twice as many injuries are reported, originating from drilling operations than from production work over a five year period (Table 2.6). In the U.K. sector the information is presented in more detail that is, by deaths, serious injury and dangerous occurrences. But still more than twice as many incidents are reported during drilling activity than production work (210 versus 84 in the 5 year period 1980–1984). However, figures for maintenance and crane activity are reported separately (a total of 212 and 227 incidents respectively) and although these could have occurred on either drilling or production installations, and also include incidents on supply boats, informed comment suggests that the higher level of activity on drilling operations would account for the larger proportion of these reported events. A detailed examination of the available information would be necessary to verify this suggestion, but it would appear from the figures already presented that drilling activity is the more hazardous activity and may be a potentially more stressful environment.

In addition to identification of psychosocial and occupational sources of stress, the decision was made to measure mental health (Crown Crisp Experiential Index), job satisfaction (Warr, Cook & Wall, 1979) and various health behaviours, including accident rate and illness. The prevalence of Type A coronary prone behaviour, and perceived level of control (locus of control) were also examined as personality variables, which may be moderators of the response to stress at work. Thus, the final objectives of this investigation were seen as:

(1)   To identify sources of psychosocial and occupational stress among offshore workers on drilling rigs and production platforms: that is, to ascertain which, if any, aspects of the way of life give rise to subjectively experienced feelings of stress.

(2)   To compare the reported degree of job satisfaction among offshore workers with that of normative groups. Also, to compare the reported degree of job satisfaction among:
   (a)   drilling rig and production platform crews,
   (b)   production platform workers employed in the U.K. and Dutch sectors.

(3)   To compare measures of mental health with that of normative groups. Also to compare measures of:
   (a)   mental health of drilling rig personnel with production platform employees,
   (b)   mental health among production platform workers in the U.K. and Dutch sectors.

(4)   To examine the coronary prone behaviour pattern of offshore workers as an occupational group, and in relation to those of the general public. Also, to compare the coronary prone behaviour pattern of:
   (a)   drilling rig and production platform personnel,
   (b)   production platform personnel in the U.K. and Dutch sectors.

(5)   To examine the measure of perceived experience of control among offshore workers, in relation to normative measures.
   (a)   Also, to examine any differences among drilling rig and production personnel.
   (b)   Between production personnel in the U.K. and Dutch sectors.

(6)   To investigate differences, if any, between the reported incidents of accidents offshore among drilling rig and production platform personnel. Also, to see if any differences in job satisfaction level, overall mental health, locus of control and Type A behaviour exist between the group involved in accidents versus those who have not been involved in an accident offshore.

(7)   To analyse the relationship, if any, between a dependent measure of:
   (a)   job satisfaction,
   (b)   mental health,
   and the independent variables of demographic, psychosocial and occupation stressors and personality behavioural measures.

7 Results

This section is a presentation of the results obtained in the investigation. Both descriptive and inferential statistics are included. The details are presented under the two main sub-headings of independent and dependent variables. The sequence used follows the research design of the survey questionnaire.

(A) Independent variables

(1) Demographic data: Frequencies count and descriptive statistics for total sample and by installation type and North Sea sector (Tables 7.1, 7.2).

(2) Psychosocial and Occupational Stressors — descriptive statistics of salient stressors (Tables 7.3, 7.4).

(3) Factor analysis of the Psychosocial and Occupational Stressors (Table 7.5).

(4) Coronary Prone Behaviour, descriptive statistics; percentage frequencies, distribution of Type A/B behaviour; comparison of Type A/Type B workers in terms of job satisfaction, mental well-being and locus of control; significant differences between offshore groups *(Tables 7.6, 7.7, Figure 7.1).

(5) Internal and external locus of control (I–E Scores), descriptive statistics, distribution of scores; statistical differences between groups and normative data (Tables 7.8, 7.9, 7.10).

(6) Health Behaviours

   (A) Accident Rate: number and percentage of incidence reported by installation type and North Sea sector (Figure 7:2). Statistical differences of group involved in accident versus no accident group for job satisfaction, overall mental health, locus of control, Type A behaviour.

*Note: As a preliminary to the computation of the independent t tests, an F-test was calculated to discover whether the assumption of homogeneity of variance was violated by the data; if it was, the t test recommended for data with heterogeneity of variance was applied.

(B) Alcohol drinking behaviour — descriptive statistics — relative frequencies.

(C) Cigarette smoking — descriptive statistics — number and frequencies for behaviour pattern, and consumption rates.

(D) Use of measures of relaxation.

(Tables 7.11, 7.11A, Figure 7.2)

(B) Dependent Variables

(1) Job Satisfaction — descriptive statistics; normative data; statistical differences between groups and normative data (Tables 7.12, 7.13).

(2) Mental Health — descriptive statistics — overall Crown Crisp Experiential Index (C.C.E.I.) scores; normative data; statistical differences between groups (Tables 7.14, 7.15).

(3) Mental Health — C.C.E.I. Sub Scores; Descriptive Statistics, Normative Data, including profile comparisons; statistical differences between groups and normative data; percentage of offshore workers scoring in the same range as psycho-neurotic out-patients (Tables 7.16 and 7.16A, Figure 7.3).

  (a) Free Floating Anxiety Table 7.17
  (b) Obsessionality Table 7.18
  (c) Depression Table 7.19
  (d) Phobic Anxiety Table 7.20
  (e) Somatic Anxiety Table 7.21
  (f) Hysteria Table 7.22

(C) Multivariate statistical analysis

To examine the relationship and dependencies observed between the dependent variables of (1) job dissatisfaction, (2) overall mental health/ mental health sub-scales and the independent variables of demographic factors; personality factors of coronary prone behaviour and internal/ external locus of control; and psychosocial and occupational stressors (Tables 7.23, 7.24).

INDEPENDENT VARIABLES

Table 7.1 Demographic characteristics of the offshore worker (oil and gas extractive industry) survey sample (N = 194)

	Number	Percentage
Age		
25 or less	39	20.1
26 – 30	51	26.3
31 – 35	34	17.5
36 – 40	31	16.0
41 – 50	35	18.0
51 – 60	3	1.5
60 plus	1	.5
Marital status		
Married	111	57.2
Remarried once	7	3.6
Remarried twice	1	.5
Living together	17	8.8
Single	45	23.2
Divorced	7	3.6
Separated	4	2.1
Widower	1	.5
Numbers of children		
None	79	40.7
One	29	14.9
Two	60	30.9
Three	21	10.8
Four or more	5	2.6
Age of children		
All pre-school age	18	9.3
Pre-school and school age	22	11.3
All school age	33	17.0
School age and post school age	25	12.9
All post school age	16	8.2
N/A	77	39.7
Level of education		
No qualifications	64	33.0
GCE O Level/CSE	60	30.9
A Level/ONC	31	16.0
HND or equivalent	28	14.4
University degree	4	2.1

Technical qualifications

83% (N = 161) identified apprenticeships, diplomas, certificates relating to skill or trade

Table 7.1 cont'd

	Number	Percentage
Job title and skill level		

A total of 44 job titles were identified within the sample — see Appendix IV for a full list of possible occupations and those identified in the survey. Levels of skill were specified as:

	Number	Percentage
Unskilled	16	8.2
Semi Skilled	46	23.7
Skilled	131	67.5

Installation type

	Number	Percentage
Production Platform U.K. Sector	90	46.4
Production Platform Dutch Sector	47	24.2
Drilling Rig Dutch Sector	46	23.7
Drilling Rig U.K. Sector* (Temporary move from Dutch Sector only)	9	4.6
Unspecified	2	1.0
(See Table 7.2 for details)		

A total of thirty-one different installations were identified and classified.

Average number of personnel on the installation

Estimates varied widely, and so the following information should only be treated as a general guide.

		Percentage
100 persons or less		54.6%
200 persons or less		29.9%
300 persons or less		13.9%
300+ persons		0.5%

Type of tour and shift pattern

	Number	Percentage
7 days on, 7 days off — only days	62	32.0
7 days on, 7 days off — alternate weeks of days and nights	17	8.8
14 days on, 14 days off — only days	13	6.7
14 days on, 14 days off — day and night shift mix	92	47.4
Others	10	5.2

Number of years worked in the offshore industry

	Number	Percentage
1 year or less	51	26.3
1 - 3	39	20.1
3 - 5	54	27.8
5 - 11	29	14.9
11 - 16	19	9.8
16+	2	1.0

(42% of sample have experience of both drilling and production operations)

Table 7.1 cont'd

	Number	Percentage
Years with present employer		
1 year or less	107	55.2
2	46	23.7
3	18	9.3
4	13	6.7
5	6	3.1
6	0	0
7	2	1.0
Last job before offshore working		
Same occupation onshore	89	45.9
Seafarer background	16	8.2
Same occupation, sea going	24	12.4
Unrelated to present occupation	59	30.4

Supervision of Others
A total of 20% (N = 39) were identified as responsible
for the supervision of others.
Mode = six persons supervised

Table 7.2 Demographic characteristics of the offshore worker (oil & gas extractive industry) survey sample by installation type (production platform or drilling rig) and by North Sea sector (United Kingdom or Dutch)

	Drilling (N = 55)		Production Dutch (N = 47)		Production U.K. (N = 90)	
	Number	Percentage	Number	Percentage	Number	Percentage
Age						
25 or less	12	21.8	9	19.1	18	20.0
26 – 30	18	32.7	9	19.1	23	25.6
31 – 35	11	20.0	6	12.8	17	18.9
36 – 40	6	10.9	6	12.8	18	20.0
41 – 50	7	12.7	14	29.8	14	16.0
51 – 60	1	1.8	2	4.3	0	0
60 plus	0	0	1	2.1	0	0
Marital status						
Married	28	50.9	24	51.1	59	65.6
Remarried – once	1	1.8	3	6.4	3	3.3
Remarried – Twice	1	1.8	0	0	0	0
Living together	5	9.1	8	17.0	3	3.3
Single	14	25.5	8	17.0	22	24.4
Divorced	1	1.8	2	4.3	0	0
Separated	5	9.1	1	2.1	2	2.2
Widower	0	0	1	2.1	0	0

Table 7.2 cont'd

	Drilling (N = 55)		Production Dutch (N = 47)		Production U.K. (N = 90)	
	Number	Percentage	Number	Percentage	Number	Percentage
Number of children						
None	24	43.6	20	42.6	34	37.8
One	13	23.6	7	14.9	9	10.8
Two	12	21.8	13	27.9	34	37.8
Three	4	7.3	7	14.9	10	11.1
Four or more	2	3.6	0	0	3	3.3
Age of children						
All pre-school age	9	16.4	2	4.3	7	7.8
All pre-school and school age	5	9.1	2	4.3	15	16.7
All school age	6	10.9	10	21.3	17	18.9
School age and post school age	9	16.4	6	12.8	9	10.0
All post school age	3	5.5	8	17.0	5	5.6
None applicable	23	41.8	18	38.3	35	38.9
Level of education						
No qualifications	18	32.7	15	31.9	31	34.4
GCE O Level/CSE	17	30.8	11	23.4	31	34.4
A Level/ONC	10	18.2	9	19.1	12	13.3
HND or equivalent	7	12.7	7	14.9	13	14.4
University Degree	2	3.6	2	4.3	13	14.4

Table 7.2 cont'd

	Drilling (N = 55)		Production Dutch (N = 47)		Production U.K. (N = 90)	
	Number	Percentage	Number	Percentage	Number	Percentage
Technical qualifications						
Cases identified with apprenticeships, diplomas, certificates relating to skill or trade	43	78.9	39	83	77	85.6
Job title and skill level						
Number of job titles identified (See Appendix IV for details of occupations)	17		19		18	
Skill level: Unskilled	5	9.1	5	10.6	6	6.7
Semi skilled	21	38.2	14	29.8	11	12.2
Skilled	29	52.7	27	57.4	73	81.1
Average number of personnel on the installation						
Estimates varied widely, and so the information should only be treated as a general guide.						
100 persons or less		94		94		10
200 persons or less		2		6		59
300 persons or less		2				30
300+ persons		0				1

Table 7.2 cont'd

	Drilling (N = 55)		Production Dutch (N = 47)		Production U.K. (N = 90)	
	Number	Percentage	Number	Percentage	Number	Percentage
Type of tour and shift pattern						
7 days on, 7 days off - only days	1	1.8	29	61.7	32	35.6
7 days on, 7 days off - alternate weeks of days and nights	2	3.6	15	31.9	0	0
14 days on, 14 days off - only days	3	5.5	0	0	9	10.0
14 days on, 14 days off - day and night shift mix	45	81.8	1	2.1	45	50.0
Others	4	7.8	2	4.3	4	4.4
Number of years worked in the offshore industry						
1 year or less	13	23.6	15	31.9	23	25.6
1 – 3	11	20.0	11	23.4	17	18.9
3 – 5	15	27.3	11	23.4	27	30.0
5 – 11	7	12.7	3	6.4	19	21.1
11 – 16	9	16.0	5	10.6	4	4.4
16+	0	0	1	4.3	0	0
	(56% of sample have experience of both drilling and production operations)		(53% of sample have experience of both drilling and production operations)		(26% of sample have experience of both drilling and production operations)	

Table 7.2 cont'd

	Drilling (N = 55)		Production Dutch (N = 47)		Production U.K. (N = 90)	
	Number	Percentage	Number	Percentage	Number	Percentage
Years with present employer						
1 year or less	27	49.1	20	42.6	60	68.7
2	15	27.3	11	23.4	20	22.2
3	3	5.5	6	12.8	7	7.8
4	6	10.9	5	10.6	2	2.2
5	2	3.6	3	6.4	1	1.1
6	0	0	0	0	0	0
7	1	1.8	1	2.1	0	0
Last Job Before Offshore Working						
Same occupation onshore	11	20.0	14	29.8	62	68.9
Seafarer background	7	12.7	7	14.9	2	2.2
Same occupation, sea going	11	20.0	7	14.9	6	6.7
Unrelated to present occupation	23	41.8	16	34.0	20	22.2
Supervision of Others						
	24% were identified as responsible for the supervision of others. Mode = 3–6 persons supervised		23% were identified as responsible for the supervision of others. Mode = 3 persons supervised		16% were identified as responsible for the supervision of others. Mode = 6 persons supervised	

Table 7.2 cont'd

NOTE 1 Drilling: Dutch Sector = 46 cases; U.K. Sector = 9 cases (temporary move to U.K. waters only). Therefore classified as one group

NOTE 2 Total Cases = 192: 2 cases unspecified by installation type.

	Drilling	Production Dutch	Production U.K.
Number of installations identified	10	16	5

Table 7.3 Psychosocial and occupational stressors — twelve highest frequencies total survey sample

1 = NO STRESS			5 = HIGH STRESS	
Position	*Variable No.*		*Mean*	*SD*
1	59	lack of paid holidays	3.734	1.497
2	57	rate of pay	3.244	1.577
3	58	pay differentials	3.163	1.613
4	55	lack of job security	3.148	1.509
5	14	last minute changes in crew relief arrangements	3.046	1.454
6	45	working with inadequately trained people	2.918	1.293
7	26	unpleasant working conditions due to noise	2.888	1.250
8	56	lack of promotion opportunity	2.840	1.409
9	46	not getting co-operation at work	2.827	1.291
10	13	working 28 days on/off	2.737	1.518
11	62	not being used to my full potential	2.707	1.398
12	21	delay in crew change due to severe weather conditions	2.691	1.363

(See appendix V.A for full details)

Table 7.4 Psychosocial and occupational stressors — percentage of respondents rating the top twelve stressors in the range 3 – 5

Position	*Variable No.*		*Percentage*
1	59	lack of paid holidays	78.3
2	57	rate of pay	64.8
3	58	pay differentials	62.2
4	55	lack of job security	65.5
5	14	last minute changes in crew relief arrangements	61.5

Table 7.4 cont'd

Position	Variable No.		Percentage
6	45	working with inadequately trained people	61.4
7	26	unpleasant working conditions due to noise	60.4
8	56	lack of promotion opportunity	58.8
9	46	not getting co-operation at work	53.5
10	13	working 28 days on/off	49.1
11	62	not being used to my full potential	53.4
12	21	delay in crew change due to severe weather conditions	49.7

Table 7.5 Factor analysis of psychosocial and occupational stressors for offshore workers in the oil & gas extractive industries — summary*

Factor 1   Relationships at work and at home (24.3% of variance)

Factor 2   Site management problems (4.8% of variance)

Factor 3   Factors intrinsic to the job (4.0% of variance)

Factor 4   The "uncertainty" element of the work environment (3.6% of variance)

Factor 5   Living in the offshore environment (3.0% of variance)

Factor 6   Safety (2.8% of variance)

Factor 7   Interface between job and family (3.1% of variance)

* Full details Appendix V.B.

Table 7.6 Descriptive statistics — independent variable Type A coronary prone behaviour

Cut off point for Type A Behaviour = 0.399
(Haynes, Feinleib & Eaker, 1981)

(Polarity: Scores >.399 = Type A Behaviour)

MEAN CORONARY-PRONE BEHAVIOUR SCORES

	N	Mean	SD
Total Sample Survey	191	.362	.196
Production Platform			
— All	136	.358	.196
— U.K. Sector	90	.376	.186
— Dutch Sector	46	.325	.213
Drilling Rig Personnel — all	55	.362	.195

PERCENTAGE FALLING INTO CATEGORIES A OR B
(Using Cut Off Point >.399 = Type A Behaviour)

	N	A	B
Total Sample	191	46	54
Production Platform			
— All	136	46	54
— U.K. Sector	90	51	49
— Dutch Sector	46	37	63
Drilling Rig Personnel	55	42	58

See Figure 7.1 for distribution of Type A/B coronary prone behaviour by installation type and North Sea Sector (percentage of total sample)

Table 7.6A Comparison of Type A and Type B workers in terms of job satisfaction, mental well-being and locus of control (using cut off point >.399 = Type A Behaviour)

	N	Means	SD	t	p*
Job satisfaction					
Type A	88	60.6	15.9	-4.38	<0.000
Type B	103	70.1	14.0		
Overall mental health (CCEI)					
Type A	88	28.0	10.3	6.61	<0.000
Type B	103	18.3	9.8		
Free floating anxiety					
Type A	88	4.9	3.2	4.34	<0.000
Type B	103	2.9	3.0		
Obsessionality					
Type A	88	6.9	3.1	5.12	<0.000
Type B	103	4.7	2.8		
Depression					
Type A	88	3.9	2.7	4.88	<0.000
Type B	103	2.1	2.4		
Phobic anxiety					
Type A	88	3.1	2.1	2.62	<0.01
Type B	103	2.3	2.1		
Somatic anxiety					
Type A	88	3.1	2.4	3.66	<0.000
Type B	103	2.0	2.0		
Hysteria					
Type A	88	6.0	3.3	3.74	<0.000
Type B	103	4.3	3.0		

Table 7.6A cont'd

	N	Means	SD	t	p*
Locus of control					
Type A	88	13.2	3.5		
				3.44	<0.001
Type B	101	11.4	4.0		

*Two Tailed probabilities

Table 7.7 Independent t tests used to test the significance of differences observed between groups — Type A behaviour (Polarity Scores >.399 = Type A Behaviour)

Production — All	134	.3664	.191	
				not significant
Drilling — All	55	.3615	.195	
(t = .16, df = 187, two tailed, p = .873)				
Production — U.K.	89	.3798	.183	
				not significant
Production — Dutch	45	.3390	.206	
(t = 1.14, df = 132, two tailed, p = .255)				
Drilling — All	46	.3431	.192	
				not significant
Production — Dutch	45	.3399	.206	
(t = .08, df = 89, two tailed, p = .939)				

Figure 7.1 Distribution of Type A/B coronary prone behaviour. Percentage of total sample, by installation type and North Sea sector

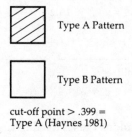

Type A Pattern

Type B Pattern

cut-off point > .399 =
Type A (Haynes 1981)

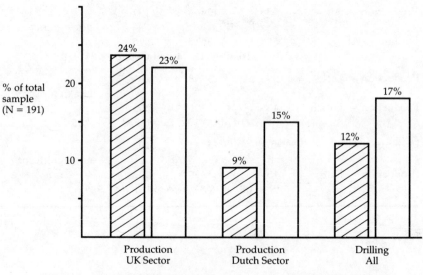

% of total
sample
(N = 191)

TYPE OF INSTALLATION AND NORTH SEA SECTOR

Table 7.8 Descriptive statistics — independent variable, personality measure — internal versus external locus of control (Rotter, (1966) I-E Scale)

Lowest Score = 0   Highest Score = 23

Polarity: Low Score = Internally Orientated
              High Score = Externally Orientated

Group	N	Mean	SD
Total sample survey	192	12.208	4.044
Production — All	136	13.338	4.074
Production — U.K.	89	12.843	4.059
Production — Dutch	47	11.383	3.585
Drilling — All	54	11.759	3.685
Normative data			
University undergraduates — U.K. sample (Gregg, 1985)	110	13.54	4.22
Coal miners — U.K. sample (age 18 — 65)	250	10.1	3.58
Combined studies by Rotter *et al.* — U.S.A. sample, 1966 (Owens, 1969)	4433	8.3	3.9
Male & female smokers (males) (average age 40.1, 13.4 years of education) (Lichtenstein & Keutzer, 1967)	95	6.59	3.65

Table 7.9 Distribution of I-E scale scores for total survey sample (N = 194) and by installation type and North Sea sector

I-E score	Total sample N = 194	Cum % frequency	Production All N = 136	Cum % frequency	Production U.K. N = 89	Cum % frequency	Production Dutch N = 47	Cum % frequency	Drilling All N = 54	Cum % frequency
23										
22										
21	1	100.0	1	100.0	1	100.0				
20	2	99.5	2	99.3	1	98.9	1	100.0		
19	4	98.5	4	97.8	3	97.8	1	99.9		
18	8	96.4	7	94.9	6	94.4	1	95.7	1	100.0
17	6	92.3	5	89.8	4	87.8	1	93.6	1	98.2
16	13	89.2	8	86.1	7	83.3	1	91.5	4	96.4
15	28	82.5	18	80.3	13	75.6	5	89.4	9	89.1
14	19	68.0	14	67.2	12	61.1	2	78.4	5	72.7
13	12	58.2	6	56.9	4	47.8	2	74.5	6	63.6
12	27	52.1	22	52.6	11	43.3	11	70.2	5	52.7
11	17	38.1	9	36.5	4	31.1	5	46.8	8	43.6
10	9	29.4	5	29.9	3	26.7	2	36.2	4	29.1
9	7	24.7	6	26.3	4	23.3	2	31.9	1	21.8
8	12	21.1	10	21.9	6	18.9	2	27.7	2	20.0
7	10	14.9	7	14.6	2	12.2	5	19.1	3	16.4
6	7	9.8	6	9.5	2	10.0	4	8.5	1	10.9
5	3	6.2	2	5.1	2	7.8			1	9.1
4	5	4.6	4	3.6	4	5.6			1	7.3
3	1	2.1							1	5.5
2	0								0	
1	1	1.5							1	3.6

	mean = 12.208		mean = 12.338		mean = 12.843		mean = 11.383		mean = 11.759	
	SD = 4.044		SD = 4.074		SD = 4.259		SD = 3.585		SD = 3.981	
	*14% internals		14% internals		11% internals		19% internals		15% internals	
	18% externals		20% externals		25% externals		11% externals		11% externals	

* Calculated within Rotter's 1966 guidelines; 16 and above = externally orientated; 7 and below = internally orientated

Table 7.10 Independent t test used to test the significance of differences observed between groups and between normative groups and survey sample: locus of control (Polarity: Higher Score — more externally orientated)

Group	N	Mean	SD
Drilling — all	54	11.759	3.685
			not significant
Production — all	136	12.338	4.074
(t =0.93, df = 188, two tailed, p = .354)			
Production — U.K.	89	12.843	4.059
			significant
Production — Dutch	47	11.383	3.585
(t = 2.07, df = 134, two tailed, p = .040)			
Drilling — Dutch	46	11.478	3.857
			not significant
Production — Dutch	47	11.383	3.585
(t = 0.12, df = 91, two tailed, p = .902)			
Normative data			
Total survey sample	192	12.208	4.044
			significant
Coal miners (Sims, 1984)	250	10.1	3.58
(t = 2.57, df = 440, two tailed, p <.02)			

Table 7.11 Health behaviours — incidence of accidents, alcohol drinking behaviour, tobacco smoking patterns, and use of relaxation methods (relative frequencies; total sample, by installation type and North Sea sector)

A Accidents

Comparison of job satisfaction, mental health and personality characteristics of individuals reporting involvement in an offshore accident leading to injury versus those individuals who remain accident free (N = 192)

	N	Mean	SD	t	p*
Job satisfaction					
Accident	46	61.913	18.218	-1.96	0.05
No Accident	146	67.048	14.589		
Overall mental health (CCEI)					
Accident	46	25.761	12.526	2.23	0.027
No Accident	146	21.603	10.532		
Free floating anxiety					
Accident	46	4.5	3.507	1.63	0.104
No Accident	146	3.603	3.166		
Obsessionality					
Accident	46	7.1087	3.129	3.78	<0.01
No Accident	146	5.1507	3.043		
Depression					
Accident	46	3.652	3.093	2.02	0.045
No Accident	146	2.733	2.563		

Table 7.11A cont'd

	N	Mean	SD	t	p*
Phobic anxiety					
Accident	46	2.456	1.929		
				-0.69	0.488
No Accident	146	2.705	2.176		
Somatic anxiety					
Accident	46	2.956	2.467		
				1.59	0.113
No Accident	146	2.349	2.183		
Hysteria					
Accident	46	5.065	3.568		
				-0.02	0.985
No Accident	146	5.0753	3.136		

* Two tailed probabilities
df = 190

Locus of control			
Accident	45	12.778	3.667
No Accident	145	11.993	3.936

(t = 1.19, df = 188, two tailed, p = .237)

A Type			
Accident	46	.4549	.214
No Accident	143	.3403	.178

(t = 3.61, df = 187, two tailed, p < .01)

* See Figure 7.2 for incidence of accidents reported — percentage of sample, by installation type and North Sea sector.

Table 7.11 cont'd

B. Alcohol Drinking Behaviour – while on shore leave time

Question 9 — Consumption rate number and frequency for total sample and by installation type and North Sea sector

Drinking Pattern	Total Sample N = 194		Production – All N = 137		Production U.K. N = 90		Production Dutch N = 47		Drilling N = 55	
	Number	Relative Frequency	Number	Relative Frequency	Number	Relative Frequency	Number	Relative Frequency	Number	Relative Frequency
(1) Teetotal	8	4.1	5	3.6	2	2.2	3	6.4	3	5.5
(2) An occasional drink	39	20.1	27	19.7	17	18.9	10	21.3	12	21.8
(3) Several drinks a week but not drinking every day	68	35.1	46	33.6	31	34.4	15	31.9	20	36.4
(4) Regularly — 1 or 2 drinks a day	33	17.0	24	17.5	14	15.6	10	21.3	9	16.4
(5) Regularly — 3/6 drinks a day	33	17.0	25	18.2	19	21.1	6	12.8	8	14.5
(6) Regularly, more than 6 drinks a day	13	6.7	10	7.3	7	7.8	3	6.4	3	5.5

(one drink is a single whisky, gin, glass of wine etc., or half-pint or bottle of beer)

C. Cigarette smoking behaviour — number and percentage for total sample and by installation type and North Sea sector

Behaviour Pattern	Total Sample N = 193		Production – All N = 137		Production U.K. N = 90		Production Dutch N = 47		Drilling N = 54	
	Number	% Frequency	Number	% Frequency	Number	% Frequency	Number	% Frequency	Number	% Frequency
Never smoked regularly	58	29.9	49	35.8	36	40.0	13	27.7	8	14.5
Have given up smoking	27	13.9	20	14.6	9	10.0	11	23.4	6	10.9
Currently smoking	108	55.7	68	49.6	45	50.0	23	48.9	40	72.7

Table 7.11 cont'd

C.2 *Average daily consumption of tobacco calculated as*
'number of cigarettes' or equivalent

Consumption rates (percentage of total sample)

Per Day	Offshore	Onshore/At Home
1 — 5	3%	7%
5 — 10	14%	12%
10 — 15	27%	30%
15 — 20	35%	27%
20 — 30	14%	19%
30 — 40	6%	3%
40 +	2%	2%

(D) Use of measures of relaxation (percentage of total sample)

		Never	Rarely	Sometimes	Often	Always
(a)	Take sleeping pills	96	2	2	0	0.5
(b)	Use tranquilisers	96	2	1	0.5	0
(c)	Smoke	49	5	17	18	12
(d)	Have an alcoholic drink	23	14	43	16	2
(e)	Drink coffee, coke or eat frequently	22	18	28	23	7
(f)	Eat junk food	53	24	17	3	0.5
(g)	Exercise *	23	22	32	17	5
(h)	Talk to someone you know	7	17	38	31	5
(i)	Use humour	11	6	38	30	13

* 55% of the sample stated that they took part in regular exercise

Figure 7.2 Incidence of accidents reported by installation type and North Sea sector — percentages

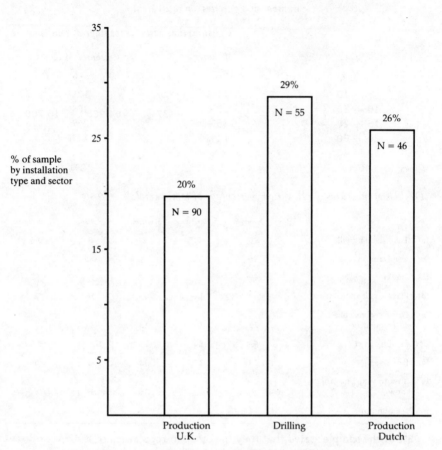

% of sample
by installation
type and sector

Total number of accidents = 24% of total sample
(N = 191)

DEPENDENT VARIABLES

Table 7.12 Descriptive statistics — dependent variable, job satisfaction (Warr, Cook & Wall, 1979)

Minimum = 16   Maximum = 112
Polarity: Lower Score — more dissatisfaction

Group	N	Mean	SD
Total sample	194	65.974	15.661
Production Platform — All	137	64.905	16.700
Production Platform — U.K. Sector	90	59.878	14.555
Production Platform — Dutch Sector	47	74.532	16.446
Drilling Personnel — All	55	68.581	12.791

Normative data (Warr, Cook & Wall, 1979)

Blue Collar Males	590	70.5	15.4

Table 7.13 Independent t tests used to test the significance of differences observed between groups and between normative groups and survey sample: job satisfaction

Polarity: Low Score — more dissatisfaction

Group	N	Mean	SD	
Drilling — All	55	68.581	12.464	
Production — All	137	64.905	16.700	not significant
				(t = -1.64, df = 129.17, two tailed, p = .103)
Production — U.K.	90	59.878	14.555	
Production — Dutch	47	74.532	16.446	* significant
				(t = -5.35, df = 135, two tailed, p = .000)
Drilling — Dutch	46	69.652	11.507	
Production — Dutch	47	74.532	16.446	not significant
				(t = -1.66, df = 82.44, two tailed, p = .101)
Total survey sample	194	65.974	15.661	
Blue Collar Males (normative group data)	590	70.5	15.4	* significant
				(t = 3.53, df = 782, two tailed, p < .01)

Table 7.14 Descriptive statistics — dependent variable, overall mental health — Crown Crisp Experiential Index

(Polarity — higher score = lower mental well-being)

Group	N	Mean	SD
Total Sample	194	22.593	11.12
Production — All	137	22.423	10.84
Production — U.K.	90	24.00	10.838
Production — Dutch	47	19.404	10.293
Drilling — All	55	22.855	11.772
Normative Data			
Industrial Workers (Males) (Crown et al., 1970)	1208	21.1	
Psycho-neurotic Outpatients (Crown, 1974)	133	44.6	
General Practice (male) (Crown & Priest, 1971)	340	22.8	

Table 7.15 Independent t tests used to test the significance of differences observed between groups — overall mental health — Crown Crisp Experiential Index

Polarity: Higher score = lower mental well being

Group	N	Mean	SD	
Drilling — All	55	22.854	11.772	
				not significant
Production — All	137	22.423	10.840	
(t = -.23, df = 190, two tailed, p = .808)				
Production — U.K.	90	24.00	10.838	
				* significant
Production — Dutch	46	19.404	10.293	
(t = 2.40, df = 135, two tailed, p = .018)				
Drilling — Dutch	46	22.261	11.532	
				not significant
Production — Dutch	47	19.404	10.293	
(t = 1.26, df = 91, two tailed, p = .211)				

Normative Data

See Table 7.14

Standard deviation scores not included in overall C.C.E.I. normative data scores. Unable to compute statistical significance of the differences between survey data and normative data mean scores.

Table 7.16 Descriptive statistics — dependent variable, mental health — sub scales, Crown Crisp Experiential Index: free floating anxiety (FFA), phobic anxiety (PHO), obsessionality (OBS), somatic anxiety (SOM), depression (DEP), hysteria (HYS)

	N	FFA		PHO		OBS		SOM		DEP		HYS	
		M	SD	M	SD	M	SD	M	SD	M	SD	M	SD
Total Sample	194	3.8	3.3	2.7	2.1	5.6	3.1	2.5	2.2	2.9	2.7	5.0	3.2
Production — All	137	3.7	3.2	2.6	2.2	5.9	3.1	2.5	2.3	2.9	2.7	4.8	3.1
Production — U.K.	90	4.3	3.5	2.5	2.0	6.1	3.0	2.7	2.5	3.4	2.9	4.9	3.2
Production — Dutch	47	2.5	2.2	2.9	2.4	5.3	3.4	2.0	1.9	2.1	2.0	4.6	2.8
Drilling — All	55	4.0	3.3	2.6	1.9	5.1	3.2	2.6	2.1	2.9	2.8	5.6	3.5
Normative Data													
Industrial — male (Crown et al., 1970)	1208	3.1	2.6	2.3	2.1	6.7	3.0	3.8	2.7	2.5	2.4	2.7	2.6
Psycho-neurotic outpatients — male (Crown, 1974)	133	9.7	3.9	5.3	3.5	8.7	3.5	8.0	3.8	7.7	3.8	5.2	3.4
General Practice (Crown & Priest, 1971)	340	2.8	2.8	2.8	2.2	6.8	2.8	4.3	3.0	3.2	2.3	2.9	2.7

Table 7.16A. Percentage of Offshore Workers scoring as high, or higher than psycho-neurotic outpatients

Measure	Psycho-neurotic outpatients Crisp (1977) mean score	Percentage of sample scoring as high, or higher
Free floating anxiety	9.7	5.6
Phobic anxiety	5.3	18.5*
Obsessionality	8.7	19.1*
Somatic anxiety	8.0	4.6
Depression	7.7	6.7
Hysteria	5.2	51.5*
Total score	44.6	4.0

Figure 7.3 C.C.E.I. profiles in terms of mean sub-scales of offshore workers, industrial males, and psycho-neurotic outpatients

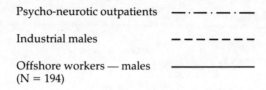

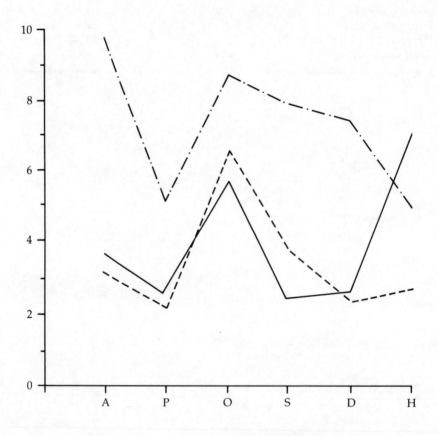

Group	N	Age	Reference
Industrial male	1208	42-56	Crown *et al.* (1970)
Psycho-neurotic outpatients — male	133	36.8 ± 13.7	Crown (1974)

Table 7.17 Independent t tests used to test the significance of differences observed between groups — and between normative groups and survey sample. C.C.E.I. sub scale: free floating anxiety (FFA)

(Polarity: High score — more anxiety)

Group	N	Mean	SD	
Drilling — All	55	4.0	3.317	
				not significant
Production — All	137	3.693	3.226	
(t = -.59, df = 190, two tailed, p = .555)				
Production — U.K.	90	4.333	3.490	
				* significant
Production — Dutch	47	2.468	2.205	
(t = 3.82, df = 130.04, two tailed, p = .000)				
Drilling — Dutch	46	3.761	3.064	
				* significant
Production — Dutch	47	2.468	2.205	
(t = 2.33, df = 81.67, two tailed, p = .022)				

Normative groups

Group	N	Mean	SD	
Total survey sample	194	3.799	3.254	
				* significant
General Practice — Males (age 35 – 70) (Crown & Priest 1971)	340	2.8	2.8	
(t = 3.59, df = 532, two tailed, p <0.01)				

Table 7.18 Independent t tests used to test the significance of differences observed between groups and between normative groups and survey sample. C.C.E.I. sub scale: obsessionality (OBS)

(Polarity: High score — more obsessional)

Group	N	Mean	SD	
Drilling — All	55	5.127	3.226	
				not significant
Production — All	137	5.869	3.131	
(t = 1.47, df = 190, two tailed, p = .143)				
Production — U.K.	90	6.156	2.979	
				not significant
Production — Dutch	47	5.319	3.369	
(t = 1.49, df = 135, two tailed, p = .138)				
Drilling — Dutch	46	5.087	3.292	
				not significant
Production — Dutch	47	5.319	3.369	
(t = -.34, df = 91, two tailed, p = .738)				

Normative groups

	N	Mean	SD	
Total survey sample	194	5.6	3.1	
				* significant
General Practice — Males (age 35 – 70) (Crown & Priest, 1971)	340	6.8	2.8	
(t = -4.45, df = 432, two tailed, p = <0.002)				

Table 7.19 Independent t tests used to test the significance of differences observed between groups and between normative groups and survey sample. C.C.E.I. sub scale: depression (DEP)

(Polarity: High score — more depression)

Group	N	Mean	SD	
Drilling — All	55	2.945	2.805	
				not significant
Production — All	137	2.956	2.689	
	($t = .02$, df $= 190$, two tailed, $p = .980$)			
Production — U.K.	90	3.4	2.894	
				* significant
Production — Dutch	47	2.106	2.013	
	($t = 3.05$, df $= 124.94$, two tailed, $p = .003$)			
Drilling — Dutch	46	2.717	2.465	
				not significant
Production — Dutch	47	2.106	2.013	
	($t = 1.31$, df $= 91$, two tailed, $p = .193$)			
Normative groups				
Total survey sample	194	2.95	2.7	
				not significant
General Practice — Males (age 35 – 70) Crown & Priest, 1971)	340	3.2	2.3	

Table 7.20 Independent t tests used to test the significance of differences observed between groups and between normative groups and survey sample. C.C.E.I. sub scale: phobic anxiety (PHO)

(Polarity: High score - more phobic)

Group	N	Mean	SD	
Drilling — All	55	2.6	1.949	
				not significant
Production — All	137	2.635	2.169	
	(t = -.32, df = 190, two tailed, p = .751)			
Production — U.K.	90	2.5	2.035	
				not significant
Production — Dutch	47	2.894	2.407	
	(t = -1.01, df = 135, two tailed, p = .315)			
Drilling — Dutch	46	2.587	2.039	
				not significant
Production — Dutch	47	2.894	2.407	
	(t = -.66, df = 91, two tailed, p = .509)			
Normative groups				
Total survey sample	194	2.655	2.113	
				not significant
General Practice — Males (age 35 – 70) (Crown & Priest, 1971)	340	2.8	2.2	

Table 7.21 Independent t tests used to test the significance of differences observed between groups and between normative groups and survey sample. C.C.E.I. sub scale: somatic anxiety (SOM)

(Polarity: High score — more somatic)

Group	N	Mean	SD	
Drilling — All	55	2.582	2.149	
Production — All	137	2.467	2.298	not significant
	(t = -0.32, df = 190, two tailed, p = .751)			
Production — U.K.	90	2.689	2.475	
Production — Dutch	47	2.043	2.186	not significant
	(t = 1.71, df = 117.98, two tailed, p = .089)			
Drilling — Dutch	46	2.391	1.903	
Production — Dutch	47	2.043	1.865	not significant
	(t = .89, df = 91, two tailed, p = .374)			
Normative groups				
Total Survey Sample	194	2.5	2.25	
General Practice — Males (age 37 – 70) Crown & Priest, 1971)	340	4.3	3.0	* significant
	(t = -7.86, df = 532, two tailed, p = <0.002)			

Table 7.22 Independent t tests used to test the significance of differences observed between groups and between normative groups and survey sample. C.C.E.I. sub scale: hysteria (HYS)

(Polarity: High score — more hysteria)

Group	N	Mean	SD	
Drilling — All	55	5.6	3.494	
Production — All	137	4.810	3.098	not significant
	(t = -1.54, df = 190, two tailed, p = .126)			

Table 7.22 cont'd

(Polarity: High score — more hysteria)

Group	N	Mean	SD	
Production — U.K.	90	4.933	3.225	
				not significant
Production — Dutch	47	4.574	2.857	
(t = .64, df = 135, two tailed, p = .522)				
Drilling — Dutch	46	5.717	3.557	
				not significant
Production — Dutch	47	4.574	2.857	
(t = 1.71, df = 91, two tailed, p = .091)				

Normative groups				
Total survey sample	194	5.06	3.24	
				* significant
General Practice — Males (age 35 – 70) (Crown & Priest, 1971)	340	2.9	2.7	
(t = 7.86, df = 532, two tailed, p <0.002)				

Table 7.23 Multiple regression analysis of psychosocial and occupational stressors, demographic, Type A behaviour and locus of control measure against overall job dissatisfaction (N = 187)

Step	Stressor variable	Multiple R	R^2	R^2 Change
1	Relationships at Work and at Home	0.539	0.291	0.291
2	The uncertainty element of the work environment	0.552	0.305	0.014
3	Factors intrinsic to the job	0.565	0.319	0.014
4	Number of children	0.576	0.332	0.013

F = 22.64
p <0.001

Table 7.24 Multiple regression analysis of job stressors, Type A behaviour, locus of control and demographic variables against overall mental health, and mental health sub-scales as obtained with the Crown Crisp Experiential Index for offshore workers (N = 187)

Step	Stressor variable	Multiple R	R^2	R^2 Change
Overall Mental Well-Being				
(1)	Type A behaviour	0.568	0.322	0.322
(2)	Relationships at work and at home	0.626	0.391	0.069
(3)	Living in the environment	0.637	0.406	0.015
(4)	Marital status	0.464	0.417	0.011
	F = 32.53 p <0.001			
Free Floating Anxiety				
(1)	Type A behaviour	0.470	0.221	0.221
(2)	Relationships at work and at home	0.574	0.329	0.108
(3)	Marital status	0.586	0.344	0.015
(4)	Living in the environment	0.596	0.356	0.012
	F = 25.132 p <0.001			
Obsessionality				
(1)	Type A behaviour	0.435	0.189	0.189
(2)	The interface between the job and the family	0.453	0.205	0.016
	F = 23.8 p <0.00			
Depression				
(1)	Type A behaviour	0.443	0.196	0.196
(2)	Relationships at work and at home	0.494	0.244	0.048
(3)	Level of education	0.511	0.261	0.017
(4)	Marital status	0.530	0.280	0.019
(5)	Age	0.541	0.293	0.012
	F = 15.0 p <0.001			
Phobic Anxiety				
(1)	Living in the environment	0.188	0.035	0.035
(2)	Number of years offshore	0.223	0.050	0.015
	F = 4.8 p <0.001			

Table 7.24 cont'd

Step	Stressor variable	Multiple R	R²	R² Change
Somatic Anxiety				
(1)	Type A behaviour	0.331	0.110	0.110
(2)	Relationships at work and at home	0.375	0.141	0.031
	$F = 15.0$ $p < 0.001$			
Hysteria				
(1)	Type A behaviour	0.352	0.124	0.124
(2)	Factors intrinsic to the Job	0.403	0.162	0.038
(3)	Number of children	0.436	0.190	0.028
(4)	Size of installation	0.453	0.206	0.015
	$F = 11.8$ $p < 0.01$			

8 Discussion

8.1 THE DEMOGRAPHIC DATA

The demographic data (Tables 7.1 and 7.2) show that the offshore worker is most commonly aged between 26-30, although the age spread is quite even throughout the early 20s and up to age 50, with only 2% of the sample aged 51+. Overall, 26% of the respondents had 1 year or less offshore experience, 28% had 3-5 years, and 26% have 5+ years experience offshore. The drilling personnel were slightly more experienced in terms of years spent offshore (29% 5+ years) and 56% of these workers had experience of both drilling and production installations, compared to the Dutch and U.K. production personnel (53% and 26% respectively).

61% of this sample were married, (including 4% remarried) with another 9% of couples living together. 23% were single, and 6% either divorced or separated. Despite a total figure of 70% married or living together, 41% did not have any children.

Previous studies have suggested that family problems are a negative consequence of offshore working, yet this study supports the findings of Sunde (1983), in Norway, that broken marriages are no more common than in the population at large. Overall, 10% of the respondents were either remarried, divorced or separated, but the figures vary somewhat, when broken down by installation type and geographical sector. Marriage breakdown rate is higher for personnel on drilling installations (14.5%) than Dutch production (12.8%) or U.K. production platforms (only 5.5%). Overinterpretation of these results should however be avoided, because of the relatively small sample sizes after breakdown by installation type and North Sea sector. As stated, the drilling rig workers do have more years offshore experience and are also more geographically mobile and less stable occupationally than the production platform work crews, and these could be contributory factors in marriage breakdown. Larger samples and longitudinal investigation would be necessary to test these assumptions.

The data show that 16% of the sample had post secondary education, and although 33% had no formal education qualifications, 83% identified technical qualifications relating to a particular trade (e.g. apprentice-ships, certificates, etc.). 20% of the respondents indicated that they were responsible for the supervision of others in some way.

The ability to cope with this way of life and offshore working, and thus vulnerability to accidents, may be related to one's previous occupation. 46% of the sample indicated the same occupation onshore prior to working in the offshore environment; 12% did the same work in a "sea-going" capacity, and another 8% had some sort of seafarer back-ground. However, 30% were currently engaged in work completely unrelated to their present occupation.

This all male sample were engaged in 44 different occupations at all skill levels (67% skilled) and were employed on thirty-one drilling and production installations in the U.K. and Dutch sectors of the North Sea. Scrutiny of such a diverse sample may therefore only be on general terms, but serves as a base to identify particular groups or areas at risk, requiring more detailed investigation. The two dominant work patterns were either, 7 days on — 7 days off, day shift only (32%); or 14 days on — 14 days off, a mixture of day and night shift working (48%). All personnel worked a minimum 12 hour shift each day spent offshore.

8.2 PSYCHOSOCIAL AND OCCUPATIONAL STRESSORS — THE TWELVE HIGHEST FREQUENCIES

Table 7.3 represents the responses drawing the twelve highest mean scores of the stressors included in the survey questionnaire (Appendix III, Section B), and Table 7.4 indicates the percentage of the sample responding to items and scoring in the 3–5 stress range. Appendix V (A) details the responses to all eighty stressors.

The oil and gas extraction industry generally depicts an image of wealth and prosperity to the outside world and so it is therefore a surprise to find the top three stressors relating to financial issues.

(1)   Lack of paid holidays
(2)   Rate of pay
(3)   Pay differentials

It would be naïve to simply take the high stress response ratings for these items on a purely face value, because the human nature of man is such that when questioned about financial reward he is surely bound to respond that it is inadequate in some way. Although there is a need to consider the simple answer to these responses, the underlying issues may be perhaps more important.

The highest scoring stressor, "lack of paid holidays", with a mean rating of 3.7 (on a 1 to 5 scale) and with 78.0% of the sample scoring 3–5 range, highlights a complex issue. Generally, offshore personnel work six months of the year on a one or two week, on-off schedule. While offshore the working week consists of seven full days of twelve hour shifts. Thus the 84 hour week is more than double that of the onshore working counterpart (commonly a 38-40 hour week over five days). So, although the offshore worker only gets paid for the time spent offshore, he theoretically is paid for 52 weeks of the year as long as he remains working.

Stress resulting from this factor of lack of paid holidays may therefore be attributed to two issues. First, one of comparison with other offshore personnel, who get annual paid holidays on a length of service entitlement and, secondly, that the offshore worker may need to take extra time off to actually get a full two week holiday away with his family. It is unlikely that the time-off period will coincide with booking/flight schedules, and time is lost in travel to and from the job, so it is necessary to take off an extra trip without pay. As one offshore worker said,

"... added to the cost of the holiday is the loss of pay, and it takes you a long time to get yourself back on your feet after that. When you see someone coming back from abroad, and he has been three times in one year, and you can't afford to go ... and you are doing the same job it makes you feel pretty bitter."

The underlying issue regarding the second highest stressor "rate of pay" (mean score 3.2) and the third highest stressor "pay differentials" (mean 3.1) has already been mentioned and is related to the "lack of paid holidays" stressor, that of comparison with others. This is an important factor and it may be responsible for a deterioration in working relationships as a result of status incongruence and reduced self esteem. Dissatisfaction and frustration with this type of situation may lead to reduced wellbeing and an increased vulnerability to accidents. The importance of effective team working has already been identified as important for successfully coping with life and work offshore (Livy & Vant, 1979), and these highly rated stressors may ultimately negatively affect working relationships in the offshore environment.

The response to the fourth highest rated stressor, "lack of job security" (mean 3.1 and 65% scoring 3–5 range), may be a further problem associated with offshore work as a "contracted" employee. In addition to the generally high levels of unemployment nationally and the instability of the industry as a matter of course, that is, rig moves in and out of the area and production platform start-up and shut-down, the contracted employee knows that the contract is for a specified period of time only, and renewal is not an automatic process, but dependent on costs and bids, and thus there is a double jeopardy. The high position rating of the item is therefore not surprising and is symptomatic of industries using contract labour both offshore and onshore. The following quote does however suggest that expectations regarding the "contractor" situation do not match reality and are thereby a resulting source of stress.

"I don't think you have a lot of security in the oil patch really ... my last Company ... I thought I was set for life ... I got 24 hours notice ... that was after seven years ... if the Company lose the contract ... then that's it, there is nothing you can do."

The element of degree of expectation features in the fifth rated highest stressor, "last minute changes in crew relief arrangements" (mean = 3.0), and item number twelve, "delay in crew change due to severe weather conditions" (mean score = 2.7). An important element in the ability to cope with stressful or unpleasant situations is a knowledge of the magnitude of the situation. Frustrating, tiring or even dangerous occurrences may be successfully coped with if the individual has a true measure of what is expected, but to be suddenly faced with having to stay and cope for a longer period of time when psychologically ready to leave is a source of stress in the offshore environment.

"a call, one or two days before, saying can you stay longer because your relief has some problems. It's OK with me ... but not one hour before the chopper takes off."

The next item rated at sixth position, "working with inadequately trained people", scored a mean stress rating of 2.9, was scored in the 3–5 range by 61% of the sample, is related to the issue of safety offshore and the acknowledgement that the environment is potentially dangerous for untrained personnel. Training is referred to in two ways. First, it may be a lack of training actually to do the particular job in question or, secondly, it may be that the skilled individual is trained to do the job in an onshore environment, but not in this unique offshore environment of drilling rigs and production platforms. This is usually on-the-job training, watching and learning from one's peers. Although many courses are compulsory within the first one or two "hitches" offshore, the system may not be sufficient to avoid putting some strain, and therefore perhaps overload, on the experienced workers who realise that it is in their own safety interests to keep an eye on the new co-worker. As one trained, skilled individual, when new to offshore life found,

"You hit the ground running ... I was assured that there would be some form of training ... but, 20 minutes after landing I was on my own ... it was quite confusing. Other guys are asked to keep an eye on you."

The seventh stressor item was that of "unpleasant working conditions due to noise" (mean score 2.9; rated in 3–5 range by 60% of the sample).

The issue of noise offshore has received considerable attention (Poulton, 1978; Jones, 1983) and although much effort has been made in areas of design to improve working conditions and protective equipment it is still rated as a high stress factor. However, it is interesting to note that the factors of noise in living accommodation did not rate as high (stressor 29, noise due to other people, mean score = 2.4; and stressor 30, noise from machinery, mean score = 2.1, although the percentage of individuals rating these items in the 3 to 5 range were 41%, and 29% respectively). This suggests that improved design to reduce noise from machinery may have been somewhat successful, although improvement is still needed.

Response to noise in the working environment may be a more complex issue which involves the social and psychological consequences of feelings of isolation, and impoverished work relationships, leading to interpersonal tension because of the constant need to wear ear plugs and ear defenders. This idea is supported by the findings of Kelly & Cooper (1981) on noise conditions among blue collar workers in the steel industry. It would seem that relatively high levels of noise offshore is a permanent feature of the offshore environment that might be reduced slightly but cannot be eliminated, and so it might be necessary to focus attention on those individuals perhaps able to cope more successfully with the lack of personal control in a high noise working environment. This will be discussed further within the section on personality as an independent variable and a potential mediator of stress at work.

"Lack of promotion opportunity" was rated eighth (mean score of 2.8, a score in 3–5 range by 59% of the sample), and may be an issue that is in part symptomatic of the industry at the present time. Competitive oil and gas prices in world markets, and high taxation, has resulted in a recession and a slight reduction in activity in the exploration for resources of oil and gas in the North Sea (but is a situation that is currently improving). Although the actual numbers employed offshore continues to rise annually it is at a reduced rate because most companies have included head-count reductions in their cost control budgets, to meet the demands of the recession. To a certain extent, changes in technology have also aided this manpower reduction. Change in technology also affects promotion opportunity in other ways. The ideology of the industry in the 1960s and early 1970s was such that an individual could promote up through the system by showing aptitude and a keen interest and would be sent for any necessary training. A competitive jobs market and a sometimes necessary increasingly higher level of education is now demanded for many offshore occupations and means that it is less easy to be promoted through the ranks. More research is necessary to establish whether contractor personnel are penalised more than operator personnel in opportunity for promotion, or whether recent changes have affected all equally. As expected, individuals are divided into those who definitely do not want any promotion if it means more responsibility, and those who do, and will experience stress because they feel, "a lack of getting anywhere ...... it all seems to be a dead end".

The ninth stressor "not getting co-operation at work" (mean score = 2.8; scored in 3–5 range by 53% of sample) is again related to the issue of poor interpersonal relationships at work and the importance of the need for effective team working. It is therefore a problem of ineffective on-site management. Frequent changes among work crews/teams, status incongruence and conflicting roles resulting from the need to meet uncompromising demands (for example, productivity levels versus safety standards), and may all be part of this perceived lack of co-operation, which is a source of stress in the offshore environment. As one individual said, "co-operation saves lots of problems". And another:

"Some individuals just don't seem to want you to show them an easier or a safer way. It makes life difficult because it might be my neck as well as theirs."

The next item, ranked number ten, is the stressor, "working 28 days on, 28 days off" (mean score = 2.74; scored in 3–5 range by 49% of the sample responding). Although this item was only considered relevant to 19% of the total sample, it is a source of stress to almost half of those exposed to it. From the interview data it is clear that some individuals enjoy this type of working, because it also means that they have long uninterrupted periods of free time. Others suggest that it is not possible to maintain the 12 hour shift, 7 days a week, for such a lengthy period of time, on some of the more arduous offshore occupations. Fatigue and decreased vigilance is likely to result in poor performance and increased vulnerability to accidents.

"You can't do your work properly anymore, after 14 days you are finished; and when you can't concentrate ... that's when you get accidents."

The final issue in this top twelve listing is the stress associated with "not being used to one's full potential" (mean score = 2.7, scored in 3–5 range by 50% of the sample responding). Some individuals do not want any changes or increased responsibility and are quite content to continue in their present roles. Others quite obviously feel that their skills or training are not being fully utilised. As one welder indicated:

"I would like to get off my tools ... maybe become an inspector, or a supervisor ...

take some more courses if need be .... but at the moment it's boring and ... well ... I've become highly skilled to do nothing ... I feel robbed".

And another,

"it's frustrating and boring now ... don't need to think ... just go out and put your donkey head on for the week."

8.3. FACTOR ANALYSIS OF PSYCHOSOCIAL AND OCCUPATIONAL STRESSORS FOR OFFSHORE WORKERS IN THE OIL AND GAS EXTRACTIVE INDUSTRIES

To reduce the number of psychosocial and occupational stressors in the survey questionnaire (Appendix III, Section 8) in order to ascertain the underlying thematic variables and to examine any interrelationships existing between the stressors, a factor analysis, using the Statistical Package for the Social Sciences (S.P.S.S., Nie *et al.*, 1975) was carried out. This is also a preparatory measure prior to regression analysis.

Factor analysis is a powerful data reduction method. Given an array of correlation coefficients for a set of variables, factor-analytic techniques reveal the existence of underlying patterns of relationships in such a way that the data may be rearranged or reduced to a smaller set of factors or components that may be taken as source variables accounting for the observed interrelations in the data (Nie *et al.*, 1975). Calculation of appropriate measures of association (product-moment-correlation) on the given set of stressors (Appendix III, Section B) produces a correlation matrix. From this, data reduction possibilities are explored and new sets of composite variables are defined. This method, known as principal component analysis, extracts orthogonal factors, on the basis of the "best" linear combination of the variable and thereby accounting for more of the variation in the data as a whole than other linear combination of variables. Second and subsequent components are also defined in the same manner, being the linear combination of variables that accounts for the most residual variance after the effect of the first component is removed from the data, and until all the variance is exhausted (Nie *et al.*, 1975).

For the purpose of this relatively small scale study factor analysis, it was necessary to incorporate all non-applicable answers (NA) into the category 1, no stress rating. Maintaining the "NA" category, which could only be treated as a missing value within the parameters of the S.P.S.S. system, resulted in the rejection of most cases because an incomplete data set was not available for many individuals. The problem featured mainly on the stressor items which related to varying shift patterns, and those of married status (Questions 9–13, 59 and 61–67). Clearly many individuals had no experience with these issues and rightly chose the option to answer "non-applicable". The options were, either to remove these items from the list of stressors or to continue the analysis by looking at specific groups, for example, by marital status, or by shift work pattern. This was not considered to be a satisfactory arrangement because of the small numbers involved, and the ultimate objective was an intention to investigate the extent to which the offshore workers are experiencing stress in their lives as a group. It is not known to what extent the items would be rated as stressors if the individual had experience of the particular situation; but it should be stated that this transfer of rankings from the "NA" to the "1", no-stress condition, does not reflect any assumptions of what might happen. It is purely a method to facilitate calculation in order to discover the psychosocial and occupational stressors of this particular work group. The use of much larger samples would not be affected by this N/A category of response.

The rotated orthogonal-factor matrix technique was utilised and produced seven major thematic factors which would be used in regression analysis and source variance. Criteria for the significance of factor loading was accepted at .209, the 1% significance level for Pearson Product-Moment Correlation Coefficients, N=150 (Child, 1976, Appendix B). A Scree test (Cattell, 1967, cited Child) was used to identify the optimum number of factors to avoid intrusion of non-common variance.

49.7% of the variance was accounted for by the seven factors derived from the analysis. Table 7.5 provides a summary of the factors, and full details are included in the Appendix V (B). The label given to each factor is based ultimately on subjective judgement, but is the product of an interpretation of an underlying theme suggested by the component parts which make up the factor (Appendix V (B)).

Factor 1 — "Relationships at Work and at Home"

"Relationships at work and at home", is the descriptive title chosen for this factor which accounts for 24.3% of the total variance. The variables that constitute the make-up of the factor may be discussed under two separate headings, but with the understanding that it is the interactive element of the total combination that ultimately produces the one single stress factor. Thus the "relationships at work" includes high stress related to, "deterioration in working relationships after intensive periods together" and, "the relationship between the Contractors and the Company men". These are indications of a general awareness of the importance of being able to get along together.

The negative consequences of a deterioration in work relationships have already been pointed out: "We eventually get on each other's nerves ... some of the younger crew get pretty depressed." And,

"I personally don't have any problems, but some of the guys say that being only a contractor ... well, makes them feel second class, and they don't like it ..."

Stress associated with relationships at home is indicated by variables such as, "problems unwinding when I return home", "disruption of my social life" and, "being unable to get involved in the community at home". The interactive quality of these stresors is accentuated by the stressor variables, "feeling isolated from home and world events while I am offshore", and "difficulties concentrating on work when my mind is thinking about home", and "feeling trapped into offshore work because no suitable onshore work is available".

"There is no doubt about it, you do miss things and it always seems to work out that something you wanted to attend is when you are out there ... then you might sit at home for a week and nothing is happening."

And,

"I really like to work as safe as possible ... sometimes you are miles away with your mind ... or you get so ... [engrossed] ... in doing the job good ... you forget the simplest rules ... and then ... boomf!!"

Or,

"I like to play rugby, but you can't belong to a club when you work 14/14 ... But I suppose the best thing about life at the moment ... is ... well, I've got a job ..."

The problem of "overspill" and response to a stressor is obvious. Stress resulting from poor relationships at work may be problematic in that the outcome may be the cause of a deterioration in relationships at home, and vice versa, if the individual cannot successfully compartmentalise problem areas of his life. However, it must be acknowledged that good relationships in one area can help to mitigate poor or unsatisfactory conditions in another area. This idea of social support as a buffering system has intuitive common-sense appeal. As House (1981) suggests, social support from a spouse may reduce the impact of job dissatisfaction on health. It may also be true that good working relationships, the support of one's peers and supervisors, is also likely to be a buffer against poor social relationships at home and an escape from the possible pressures of family living and responsibilities.

Factor 2 — "Site Management Problems"

This accounts for 4.8% of the total variance. The constituent parts, "not getting co-operation at work", "inadequate instruction to do the job", "frequent changes in my work crew/team", "having no-one to talk over problems with" and, "problems arising because of language/dialect difficulties", reflect this title quite accurately. In the main, the stress response seems to be related to the fact that the individual cannot do the job in question to a personally safe and satisfactory degree, for some reason that could be solved by effective, on-site management.

"If you have a good driller, it makes for a good atmosphere amongst the whole crew ... but a moody, uncertain guy who can't put his point over ... is not easy to work for."

"... the roustabouts don't crew change at the same time ... it would be easier to have the same crew for the two weeks ... you can tell how they are going to work and react and it just makes life easier ... the same with the crane driver ... he is a pretty important person and it helps to know what he is like, reactions and timing and so on ... simultaneous change-over for the whole crew would be better."

It may also be that the 20% of this sample who reported that they were responsible for the supervision of others (Table 7.1), experience distress at "having to discipline people". Both working and living in close proximity, for extended periods of time, may aggravate this situation, which is related to the "good relationships" factor previously discussed.

It would seem to be a paradox to suggest that, "having no-one to talk over problems with" is a source of stress for individuals living and working with 40–350 other individuals in an offshore environment, especially when "lack of privacy" is also rated as a stressor. A potentially stressful situation may arise because the only people to talk to are the individuals that one must live and work with in close proximity for long periods of time. Culturally, weakness is not generally expressed, and one would suppose that this is even more so the case in the "macho", mainly all male, environment of the oil and gas extractive industry. Thus an individual with a problem may feel that he cannot discuss a matter with either a co-worker or the boss. This problem may be enhanced for contracted personnel who do not have a company representative as a supervisor offshore, and answer directly to the operators in charge. To reveal any problems that might be seen as potentially responsible for reduced work performance may pose a threat to the individual's job prospects offshore.

"If you have a good medic on board it's possible to talk to him ... well you see ... he is not exactly in the immediate work environment ... so that's OK ... and this one is very good."

Factor 3 — "Factors Intrinsic to the Job"

Accounting for 4.0% of the total variance this mostly speaks for itself when the components are examined. It may be reviewed mostly under three basic headings; shift work patterns, physical conditions and travel related to the job. Constituent variables relating to shift working patterns include, "working 7 days on/off — alternate weeks days and nights", "working 14 days on/off — days" and, "working 28 days on/off". Although the numbers working these more unusual patterns are small, they are apparently a source of stress. As expected within this blue collar group the actual physical conditions of the working environment featured strongly, with constituent factors such as, "unpleasant working conditions due to heat, cold, vibration and noise". The issue of "vibration" in the offshore environment would appear to be an important item in terms of sources of stress, as "disturbance in living accommodation due to vibration and noise from machinery" also featured in this factor. Travel related to the job is expressed as a source of stress by the variable "staying overnight to meet early check-in time". This reduces the time-off period of the individual and is thus not surprisingly a source of stress. The stress of "last minute change in crew relief arrangements" is, in one respect, a sense of powerlessness at the hands of the severe weather conditions, but in another, it is annoyance and frustration with the time management situation, which they also see as beyond their control, but a situation which they believe could be improved upon.

Factor 4 — "The Uncertainty Element of the Work Environment"

3.6% of the total variance. Expression of this source of stress is through issues such as, "working with inadequately trained people", "inadequate specific training for offshore work", "having to work with people unsuited to offshore life and work" and, "mixing and working with people from different countries". This is perhaps related to the "safety" factor in the offshore environment, where such "uncertainties" may lead to increased vulnerability to accidents.

"Some just can't stand it ... you can see in their faces."

"The young guys ... they are a different breed ... after an apprenticeship ... they think they know it all ... they turn up out here and you feel obliged to 'educate' them."

"The ex-seamen have a respect for the sea and these conditions ... you know what to expect and I'm used to being away from home ... so yes, it helps me when I'm out there for two weeks ... that's nothing."

The stress associated with "mixing and working with people from different countries" is also part of this uncertainty element in the environment. There is no doubt that many individuals find this to be stimulating and an interesting aspect of their job, but it may at the same time be a strain on the individual. Thus, coping with cultural differences of the many different nationalities working in the North Sea offshore industry, may be a potentially stressful situation. The last survey, September 1984, indicates a total of 52 different nationalities in the U.K. sector of the North Sea and so coping with frequent change in work crew/teams may also extend to coping with a change in culture and language as well as the many different ways of working.

"I get mad when I know they can speak English, but won't ... we try to avoid misunderstanding ... but some of the dialects are difficult."

And,

"In our crew we had German, Norwegian, English and American ... and me ... I like it ... it's interesting ... but, sometimes the English speaking people can be 'put out' ... and don't, or won't understand that they have to speak more slowly."

The financial issues, such as "rate of pay" and "pay differentials" are problems unique to the contractor working offshore. Uncertainty and the stress that results are no doubt the product of insecurity about the future. Contractors live and work in the knowledge that their services are only required for a set period of time for a given rate of pay, and this will fluctuate as future contracts are won or lost.

The issue of "women working offshore" appeared in this factor of uncertainty. As one man, who had worked in an onshore environment with women said,

"Women offshore ... will cause some problems, I suppose ... change the macho image somewhat ... and be disturbing for a start. I guess it would be OK after a while."

Factor 5 — "Living in the Offshore Environment"

At 3.0% of the total variance, this is also a label that is easily applied to the factor when the components are examined, "sharing living/sleeping accommodation", "disturbance in living accommodation due to noise from other people and heat and/or cold", and "lack of privacy". Taken together these items convey a sense of the way of living in these unique offshore conditions, and as Livey and Vant (1979) suggest, the life is not for everyone. As one individual explained:

"Our 4 man cabin usually has three guys sleeping at any one time. There has to be an awareness of other people ... try not to develop any anti-social habits ... the biggest thing about working offshore is that you don't have any privacy and it's difficult to be alone for any length of time."

And,

"The guy I share with just can't sleep the first few days ... I get disturbed ... he has always got the light on ... as soon as he gets into it ... it's OK."

Factor 6 — "Safety"

Accounting for 2.8% of the total variance safety is the simple label given to the sixth factor. The constituent variables reflect this title quite clearly: "I feel that my own and others safety is at risk if I make a mistake", "feeling inadequate when someone has an accident", and "lacking confidence about medical facilities". Having to wait for a trained medic to arrive on the scene and being unable to help is a source of stress in the environment. Although there is a great deal of faith and confidence in the rig medics in general, some doubt exists regarding the ability to cope with a serious accident. Some feelings exist that the issue of safety offshore is a "political" thing and that, "a lot of lip service is paid to safety ... going through the motions because legislation is laid down". Others believe, "you have got to look after yourself". Resentment is also evident regarding the "obsessional" attitude of some companies towards the issue of safety.

"Sometimes it just gets to be a pain ... they overdo it ... you know how it is ... sometimes I think that it's too much ... and well ... has an inverse effect of what you want ... you get turned-off."

This however may be more of a reaction to the fact that the individual is not allowed to repress fears about the special risks associated with the hazardous environment of the North Sea, because of the continual emphasis on safety.

Other individuals have the idea that if you need to think about hazards and safety all the time, then it is the time to quit and go ashore. As Bohemier (1985) believes, it is human nature to avoid thinking about danger and to a certain extent some of this is necessary to cope with the realities of the way of life. Maintaining a balance in safety training is clearly the important issue.

The other variables incorporated in this "safety" factor is the stress associated with "keeping up with change and new equipment" and "long periods of intense concentration". This is perhaps related to the fears associated with the risk to safety as a result of making a mistake, or being unsure about coping with new methods, systems or equipment because of fatigue and the inability to concentrate when tired.

Finally, the stress of "travel by helicopter" formed part of this factor, and 27% of the respondents rated this item in the 3–5 stress level range. This supports the Norwegian sector findings (Sunde, 1983). In fact, the need to travel by helicopter was actually the most commonly reported reason for quitting offshore work in the Norwegian sector of the North Sea.

Factor 7 — "Interface Between Job and Family"

This accounts for 2.6% of the total variance, and again is fairly explicit in that it refers quite distinctly to the issues that are a source of stress for individuals working away from the home and family environment for regular periods of time. Variables incorporated within this factor include, "working in an all male environment", "leaving your wife/partner to cope/make decisions", "feeling threatened by wife/partner's independence", "wife/partner's attitude to me working offshore" and "risk of marriage breakdown because I work offshore". Related to these is the constituent variable of "restricted ability to contact home while I am away". However, this reduced communication, seen as a source of stress, may be perhaps a blessing in disguise. The restricted opportunity to contact home may add to a stress situation in that the individual is unable to discuss any problems, but he is also protected from problems at home, but which are situations that he cannot do anything about while he is offshore. Knowledge of a situation in which one feels powerless may be the more damaging source of stress. As one individual said,

"I don't like phoning home when I'm on a rig ..., 'cause if it's bad news, you just go to pieces out there and get upset ... and I can't do anything."

Disturbing news from home may result in reduced concentration and therefore increased vulnerability to accidents.

8.4. INDEPENDENT VARIABLE — CORONARY-PRONE BEHAVIOUR

In section five, characteristics of the person were discussed as individual modifiers of the response to stress. An important modifier may be the Type A coronary-prone behaviour pattern. Identification of this predisposition to respond in a certain way and its association with an increased risk of heart disease is well documented. The behaviour pattern is characterised by restlessness, haste, extreme competitiveness, hard driving, a distinct sense of time urgency, hostility and aggression. To investigate the prevalence of the Type A behaviour pattern in the offshore environment the short questionnaire "The Framingham type-A behaviour scale" was included in the survey.

The Type A scores were calculated and are detailed in Table 7.6; the mean score for the total group (.362) and by installation type (that is "production" versus "drilling") and by North Sea sectors (U.K. versus Dutch) are also included. A comparison between the scores of the different groups shows that there are no significant differences observed (Table 7.7, details of t tests).

The percentage falling into the categories of either Type A or Type B were also calculated (Table 7.6), and as a total group they mostly conform to the expected norm of a 50:50 split (Haynes *et al.*, 1981) with 46% of the total sample identified as Type A and 54% as Type B individuals. This categorisation is based on the criteria cut-off point of $>.399 =$ Type-A pattern (Haynes *et al.*, 1981). However, an interesting difference is observed when percentages are calculated by installation type and sector. The "production-all" group does not differ from the norm, that is 46% and 54%, A and B types respectively. But, when these are identified by geographical sector, a different pattern emerges.

Production — U.K.	51% Type A	49% Type B
Production — Dutch	37% Type A	63% Type B

And for the drilling group the pattern observed is 42% Type A and 58% Type B. Figure 7.1 shows the distribution of Type A/B behaviour as a percentage of the total sample.

It is suggested that the higher prevalence of Type B individuals in the Dutch sector (note that the drilling is mainly all Dutch personnel) might be due to three factors.

(1)   There is something inherently different about the Dutch as a nation, versus United Kingdom residents.

(2)   A self-selection system is in operation in the offshore environment. As Caplan *et al.* (1975) suggests, individuals may be attracted to an industry for various reasons but self-select out as individuals more suited stay over a period of time. Type A individuals may be attracted to the industry with its unique image of perhaps adventure and even glamour, but it may be the Type Bs who stay longer and are more satisfied and maintain a better mental wellbeing than the As who become disillusioned and less able to cope with the ultimate routine of shift work and long hours offshore (this will be discussed in more detail in the sections on job satisfaction and

mental health). However, larger sample sizes would be necessary to test this assumption.

It is also suggested that previous occupational background data may support a "self-selection" hypothesis. A total of 33% of the drilling personnel, and 30% of the Production—Dutch sector have seafarer experience prior to working offshore, compared to only 9% of the Production—U.K. sample (Table 7.2), and this may explain the higher percentage of Type Bs in the Dutch sector of the North Sea.

Philbert *et al.* (1975) suggests that a sea-going past history is an asset in coping with the life and conditions in the offshore environment. Not the least of these is the actual issue of being away from the home environment for an extended period of time. However, there is a third possibility to consider.

(3) Type A is a style of behaviour and an habitual response to circumstances. It is therefore a behavioural predisposition and a potent conditioning variable, thus a work environment can elicit and reinforce this pattern of behaviour. It may therefore follow that individuals may become less of Type A, or more Type B, over time. The comparison of groups by age and number of years' experience offshore is not possible with this small sample, and cross sectional studies of this type are weak in that it is not possible to control all intervening variables. Ideally, longitudinal research is needed to discover the extent to which Type A behaviour is inherent or learned.

Although a more detailed breakdown by installation type and North Sea sector is not possible, some interesting differences are observed when the total sample is divided into Type A or Type B categorisations. Table 7.6A shows that Type As are much less satisfied with their jobs ($t = -4.38, p < 0.000$) and have a significantly lower overall mental well being ($t = 6.61, p < 0.000$) than Type Bs. Mental health sub-scale scores indicate they are much more anxious, obsessional, and depressed. They have higher hysteria scores and higher levels of phobic and somatic anxiety than Type B individuals. (It is important to remember, that as an occupational group, scores for obsessionality and somatic anxiety were lower than for comparable onshore populations Tables 7.18 and 7.20.) Type As also appear to be significantly more "externally orientated" than their Type B counterparts (locus of control mean score of 13.2 compared to Type B mean score of 11.4, $t = 3.44, p < 0.001$). This result is conflicting in that Type As usually like to be in control of a situation. However, it is also very important to observe that 36% of individuals identified as Type

A report having an accident leading to injury, whereas only 13% of Type Bs report being involved in such an incident.

Thus the relevance or importance of an understanding of this personality variable in terms of the offshore industry may be in the short term consequences rather than the long term consequences of increased risk of C.H.D. Although this should not be underestimated nor over-looked, the C.H.D. risk-factor situation is still not clear for blue-collar worker groups (Kasle, 1978) and more research is needed. However, in the short term there is a need to consider the possibility of increased vulnerability to accidents. This may be as a direct consequence of the Type A behaviour pattern of haste and time urgency. Also, "aggression", a characteristic of Type A individuals, is another trait which is tentatively proposed (but not statistically proven) as likely to lead a person to being involved in an accident (Oborne, 1982). There is also a degree of similarity between the Type A person and the "extrovert" (Eysenck, 1947), described as an individual who craves excitement, impulsive, prefers to keep moving and who is aggressive. Research suggests that the individual scoring high on extraversion is more likely to have been involved in a recorded accident or driving violation (Fine, 1983; Mackay *et al.*, 1969). Thus it follows that the Type A individual may be more likely to be involved in an accident offshore. Indirectly, an accident may occur because the Type A individual is attracted to the industry, but gradually suffers job dissatisfaction and a reduced mental wellbeing, but is forced to stay in the environment because there is no onshore job alternative. The consequence of this might be an increased vulnerability to an accident.

An examination of the accident records for this group of offshore workers (Figure 7:2) shows that 24% of the total have had an accident at some stage in their offshore career, a total of 46 incidents. A breakdown by installation type and sector shows that:

Production — U.K.   a total of 18 incidents; 20% of the sample (N=90)
Production — Dutch   a total of 12 incidents; 26% of the sample (N=46)
Drilling   a total of 16 incidents; 29% of the sample (N=55)

These figures are in accordance with the statistics reported for the North Sea area in general (Tables 2.5, 2.6) where incidents of death, serious injury and dangerous occurrences are all more prevalent on drilling installations than production platforms.

Although the numbers are small, the prevalence of B Types in the Production—Dutch and the Drilling sectors do not appear to have any significant difference on the number of accidents offshore. However, a calculation of Type A scores for the individuals involved in an accident

(N=46) versus those not involved (N=146) produced mean scores of .455 and .340 respectively. Thus those involved in accidents rate as Type As with the criteria set by Haynes *et al.* (1981), and those in the no-accident group rate as Type Bs. Comparison of these mean scores shows a significant difference (t=3.61, df=187, two tailed, p <0.01) (Table 7.11A): as it therefore appears that individuals with Type A behaviour patterns are also more likely to have been involved in an accident than their Type B counterparts, this is an issue which warrants further attention. A retrospective study of this nature does not permit statements regarding "causation" to be made. So, from this survey, it is not known whether involvement in an accident "causes" the behaviour pattern, or whether the Type A individual is more vulnerable to an accident in this particular environment.

However, it is not possible to simply consider only one personality characteristic as a mediator of stress in the environment. Other variables will also interact and account for a share of the variance in a situation; one of these is "locus of control", and this will be discussed next.

8.5. INDEPENDENT VARIABLE — LOCUS OF CONTROL

As indicated in Section 5 the personality characteristic of "locus of control" (Rotter, 1966) may be an important moderator of stressors in the environment. It refers to the degree of "control" perceived by the individual in a given situation. The rationale for including this measure in the survey is to examine the distribution of individuals rated as either "internals" or "externals" in the offshore environment. Rotter (1966) believes that "internals" should suffer more in the extremely noisy offshore environment, which they are unable to control, or a self-select situation may operate and so a prevalence of "externals" will be found in the population. Yet, if noise is not a major concern, "internals" will cope significantly better than externals. However, as Lefcourt (1979) warns, locus of control is not a trait nor a typology and people are not totally internals or externals.

Scores were calculated for the total sample and for each group by installation type and geographical sector. Table 7.8 provides the details of the means and standard deviations obtained The main focus of interest was to observe any differences across the various groups. As can be seen from Table 7.10 no significant differences were observed, except between the U.K. Production and the Dutch Production groups (with mean scores of 12.8 and 11.4 respectively) (t=2.07, df=134, two tailed, p=.040). A comparison with normative data proved difficult due to the general lack of data available for British Norms and for blue collar workers in particular. However, an observation comparison of mean scores shows that this group of workers (mean score = 12.2) are appreciably more external than the composite mean score of mainly U.S.A. students, produced by Owens (1966) from Rotter's early studies (N=4,433, means=8.3). Gregg (1985) suggests that these scores, derived in the 1960s, are too low and that individuals are now more "external" generally. Later research (late 1970s) produces mean scores of around 9.50 to 11.0. A recent study (Gregg, 1985) with university students produced an extremely high score of externality (13.5), whereas it would be expected that students would be the more internal (Otten, 1977). A comparison with a U.K. sample of coal miners (Sims, 1984) was possible, and the mean score of 10.1, compared with this offshore group, with a mean score 12.2 proved to be significant (Table 7.10, t=2.57, df=440, two tailed, p <.02).

Using the criteria set by Rotter (1966) the distribution of scores was examined (Table 7.9) to identify the percentage of internals and externals within the various groups.

	A score of 7 or less	A score of 16+
Total Sample	14% internal	18% external
Production — all	14% internal	20% external
Production — U.K.	11% internal	25% external
Production — Dutch	19% internal	11% external
Drilling	15% internal	11% external

Bearing in mind that noise at work rated seventh in the top twelve list of stressors, with 60% of the sample rating it in the 3–5 stress range, it would seem likely that externally orientated individuals would predominate in the offshore environment.

This pattern is, however, only found among the U.K. Production group, and it is interesting to note that this is also the group of workers with the lowest rate of accidents (20% of the sample, compared to 29% of drilling rig personnel, and 26% of Dutch production employees, Figure 7.2).

However, it is necessary to examine data by "occupational group" in the offshore environment, before any firm conclusions may be made about the possible relationship between the personality variable "locus of control" and the degree of exposure to noise at work and coping strategies. This also would require a more detailed analysis of both objective and subjective reports of noise conditions for each occupational group.

The final analysis carried out in this section on locus of control was to examine the mean scores of the accident versus no accident group (Table 7.11A). Scores of 12.78 and 11.99 were recorded respectively, and compared, and no significant difference was observed.

8.6. DEPENDENT VARIABLE — JOB SATISFACTION

The Warr, Cook & Wall (1979) Job Satisfaction Scale was used to examine the strength of response among this group of offshore workers and across the group according to their installation type and geographical sector to see if any differences exist, and Table 7.12 details the mean scores obtained.

As a total group, a score of 65.97 was obtained (minimum score possible 16, maximum 112, polarity — lower score = more dissatisfaction). The only norms available for this scale, to serve as a comparison, were an industrial blue collar male sample (Warr, Cook & Well, 1979) with a mean score of 70.5. A significant difference was observed between this and the offshore workers as a group (t = 3.53, df = 782, two tailed, p <.01) (Table 7.13), thus indicating that the offshore workers are significantly less satisfied than their industrial "onshore" blue collar counterparts. In some respects, direct comparison of this nature is inappropriate because the "blue collar category" embraces many different types of industry, and thus the intention here is for the comparison to serve only as a very general guide to the degree of satisfaction or dissatisfaction that may exist. In fact, Warr *et al.* (1979) had drawn their sample from manufacturing industry only and state that service industries — construction, agriculture and mining, were excluded from their sample.

A comparison of the scores for the Drilling group, mean score 68.6, and the Production group as a whole, mean score 64.9, was not significantly different, and a comparison of scores for the Dutch Drilling group, mean score 69.6, and the Dutch Production group, mean score 74.5, did not reach significance either. However, a highly significant difference was observed between production workers in the U.K. and Dutch sectors, with mean scores respectively 59.9 and 74.5 (t = -5.35, df = 135, two tailed, p <.000), with the workers in the U.K. sector much less satisfied than the Dutch (Table 7.13).

The final part of the analysis in this section was to see if any significant difference was observed in job satisfaction scores between those individuals who had been involved in an accident offshore, and those who had not. Mean scores were 61.9 and 67.0 respectively, and were found to be significant (t = -1.96, df = 190, two tailed, p = <.05) (Table 7.11A). However, it should be remembered that although accident "victims" appear to be much less satisfied with their jobs, it is not known whether involvement in the accident leads to this state, or whether dissatisfaction is present before the event, and is in part a contributory factor. This is a weakness of this type of retrospective study.

8.7. DEPENDENT VARIABLE — MENTAL HEALTH

The Crown-Crisp Experiential Index (C.C.E.I.) was used to obtain an overall measure of general emotionality or "neuroticism". The mental ill-health of the sample was determined by computing the six sub-scales contained within this questionnaire. A summary of the overall measures obtained for the total group, and the groups by installation type and geographical sector, are detailed in Table 7.14, and sub-scale scores for free floating anxiety (A), phobic anxiety (P), obsessionality (O), somatic anxiety (S), depression (D), and hysteria (H) are given in Table 7.16, together with appropriate normative data, as a basis for comparison purposes.

The only statistically significant difference observed in overall mental well being was found between U.K. and Dutch production personnel (mean score 24.0, and 19.4 respectively), ($t = 2.40$, df $= 135$, two tailed, p $= .018$) (Table 7.15). Thus the U.K. production personnel have a significantly lower mental well being than the comparable workers in the Dutch sector. It is not possible to compute t test comparisons with normative groups for overall mental health because standard deviation measures are not supplied. Comparison by observation of mean scores indicates that as a total group, a score of 23.0 compares favourably with general practice norms of 22.8. The U.K. production personnel have the lowest mental ill-health (mean score 24.0) and the Dutch production platform workers the best (19.4).

Crisp (1977) suggests that no more than 5 to 10% of the normal population should score as high as, or higher than psycho-neurotic out-patients (mean score 44.6). Scrutiny of frequency distribution of scores for the total sample reveals a figure of 4% for individuals scoring 44 or above (Table 7.16A) and, with a lowest score of three, and a highest of fifty seven.

As a broad picture, the mean sub-scale scores for the total sample of workers are presented in the form of a profile, and compared with a normative industrial male sample, and a psycho-neurotic out-patient sample, Figure 7.3. It can be seen that the group of offshore workers score higher on free floating anxiety, and hysteria, but lower on obsessionality and somatic anxiety. Table 7.16A also shows the percentage of offshore workers scoring as high, or higher than psycho-neurotic out-patients for each sub-scale, and there is cause for concern on the scores for obsessionality and phobic anxiety. These will be reviewed individually in more detail.

Free floating anxiety

Table 7.17 indicates that there are some significant differences between the groups observed by installation type and geographical sector. The U.K. Production group are the most "anxious" (mean score of 4.3), with the Dutch Drilling personnel scoring 3.8, and the Dutch Production the least anxious, with a mean score of only 2.5. As a total group (mean score = 3.8), compared to a normative sample of industrial males (mean score = 2.8), the difference is highly significant ($t = 3.59$, $df = 532$, two tailed, p <0.01). 5.6% of the sample score 10 or more (psycho-neurotic mean score = 9.7), which is satisfactory in terms of Crisp's (1977) criteria.

Free floating anxiety does not relate to any specific cause, but is dread, tension or indefinable terror without cause or panic. The C.C.E.I. asks questions about feeling upset for no obvious reason, unease and restlessness, worrying and feeling "strung-up". This would seem to be supported by the prominence given to the stressors identified as "Problems unwinding when I return home", and "Feeling that time is passing by too quickly". Although not statistically significant, it should be noted, (Table 7.11A) that accident "victims" have a higher level of anxiety (mean score = 4.5) than accident free individuals (mean score = 3.6) ($t = 1.63$, $df = 190$, $p = .104$).

Depression

Crown and Crisp (1979) describe depression as sadness of mood, difficulty in thinking clearly and slowing of actions and activity, thus the implication for the organisation in terms of decreased performance, effectiveness, and potential increased vulnerability to accidents is obvious. As a total group, the offshore worker compares favourably to the general population (mean scores 2.9 and 3.2 respectively). The U.K. production personnel have a slightly higher level (3.4), whereas the Dutch production employees have the best mental well being in terms of depression, with a mean score of 2.1. It is important to note that accident victims are significantly more depressed (mean score of 3.65) than accident free individuals (mean score = 2.7) ($t = 2.02$, $df = 190$, $p = .045$).

Hysteria

The definition of hysteria is taken from the *Glossary of Mental Disorders* (1968), "individuals with shallow labile effectivity, and overdependence on others. These individuals crave love and attention, though being unreliable and unsteady in their personal relationships. Under stress they may develop hysterical symptoms. They tend to over-dramatise situations." However, the validity of this sub-scale is questionable and it is suggested that it is a better measure of sociability and extraversion (Crisp *et al.*, 1978).

Scores for the total sample and the Drilling group are high (mean scores 5.6 and 5.7 respectively) (Table 7.16) and the Dutch and U.K. production personnel have lower scores of 4.6 and 4.9 respectively, although these differences are not statistically significant. The total sample score (5.1) is highly significant in relation to that of the normative data for general practice males, mean score of 2.9 (t tests, Table 7.22). In fact, the score for the Drilling group (5.6) is higher than given by Crown & Crisp for psycho-neurotic out-patients (5.2); but as already discussed, it is more likely that this scale should be regarded as a measure of extraversion, sociability and youth rather than a psycho-neurotic symptoms. In fact, 51% of this relatively young sample score 5 or more on this sub-scale.

It is therefore more likely that a personality dimension is being measured and thus not the intention to interpret the high scores obtained in this sub-scale in relation to mental ill-health. It is however suggested that some consideration be given as to why the Drilling group have higher scores overall than the production platform personnel. Further research should aim to understand the issue of "self-selection" into occupations and to what extent this may prevail in the offshore environment.

Obsessionality

Crown & Crisp suggest that this means meticulousness, adherence to routine, punctuality, dislike of sudden change, need to control the environment, tendency to over-check, dislike of dirt. As a group, the offshore worker is significantly less obsessional than his onshore male counterpart, with mean scores of 5.6 and 6.8 respectively (t = -4.45, df = 432, two tailed, p <.002). No significant differences were observed between the groups by installation type and sector (t tests, Table 7.18). However, there is cause for concern when frequency data is scrutinised, in that 19% of the sample score 9 or more (8.7 mean score of psycho-neurotics). Although some of the behaviours described by Crown & Crisp would appear to be important to maintain good housekeeping and a safe environment, it may be that the environment is eliciting and reinforcing these behaviours in an over-zealous manner, to the extent that these over-obsessional individuals suffer a reduced mental well being. This behavioural tendency has not been computed by groups because of the small sample sizes involved, but is an issue to consider in further research as a possible explanation of the high free floating anxiety scores obtained. However, it is observed (Table 7.11A) that accident "victims" have a much higher level of obsessionality (mean score 7.1) compared to "accident free" individuals (mean score 5.2) (t = 3.78, df = 190, two tailed, p <0.01).

Somatic anxiety

The somatic concomitants of anxiety include breathlessness, headaches and aches and pains. The C.C.E.I. asks questions about dizziness, shortness of breath, digestive upsets, appetite loss, tiredness and exhaustion and sleep disturbance. The relevance to this survey are the questions on tiredness and exhaustion, in that individuals in the offshore environment work much longer hours than in an onshore environment, that is 12 hour shifts, 7 days a week, usually for 1 or 2 weeks without a break. It is therefore interesting and surprising that they appear to suffer less somatic anxiety than their onshore male counterpart, with mean scores of 2.5 and 4.3 respectively. There are no significant differences across the groups (t tests, Table 7.21) and only 4.6% of the sample scored 8 or more (psycho-neurotics score = 8).

These results are surprising in that the issue of insufficient sleep while offshore was rated in the 3–5 stress range by 41% of the respondents, and disturbance in living accommodation due to noise from other people featured in the stress factor number five. These unexpected results may however be explained in that the offshore worker does have an opportunity to "catch-up" during the long periods of time off and so, overall, does not feel tired or exhausted. Although the questionnaire is concerned about the way people feel or act "generally" some considera-tion must be allowed for the fact that the questionnaires were completed in the home environment onshore, and perhaps different pictures may evolve if the same questions were asked in the offshore environment, especially towards the end of a two week hitch. This, and the issue of social desirability, that is, simply not wanting to admit to tiredness etc., are the inherent weakness of this type of measure.

Phobic anxiety

Although no significant differences were found between groups off-shore and in comparison with normative data, general practice males (mean scores of 2.7 and 2.8 respectively) (Table 7.20, t tests), it is important to note that 18.5% of the total sample scored 5 or more (psycho-neurotics mean score 5.3). The weakness of this sub-scale has already been discussed, however, the common phobias asked about include phobias of enclosed spaces, heights and crowds, all issues that would be very relevant to living and working conditions in the offshore environment. It is thus perhaps a contributing factor to reduced mental wellbeing and increased vulnerability to accidents for the individual who suffers from these phobias but stays in the offshore environment because no suitable alternative employment is available elsewhere.

8.8 MULTIVARIATE ANALYSIS

Multiple regression analysis was used as a means of predicting the overall dependence of job satisfaction and mental health on the independent psychosocial and occupational stressors, coronary prone behaviour, locus of control and demographic variables. This method of analysis allows one to study the linear relationships between a dependent variable and a set of independent variables whilst simultaneously taking into account the interrelationships among the independent variables. Stepwise multiple regression using the Statistical Package for the Social Sciences was used (Nie *et al.*, 1975). The cut-off point was determined by statistical criteria laid down by Kerlinger and Pedhazer (1973). That is, the overall F ratio for the equation was at, or approaching, significance and the partial regression coefficient for the individual independent variable being added was at, or approaching, a statistically significant level ($p < .05$). Therefore the R^2 change value was acceptable at the .01 level, that is, making a contribution of not less than 1% of the total variance.

Stepwise multiple regression — overall mental health and mental health sub-scales

Overall mental health

Table 7.24 indicates that there are four factors which predict overall mental health, at a level of significance of .001 or greater. They were Type A coronary-prone behaviour; Factor 1 of the psychosocial and occupational stressors, "relationships at work and at home"; Factor 5, "living in the environment", and the demographic variable "marital status" (that is, the status of being married, or living with a partner, is a small but significant predictor of overall mental well being in the offshore environment). These predictors together account for 41% of the total variance and are therefore strongly predictive of overall mental health.

Distribution of Type A coronary-prone behaviour (Table 7.6), and the overall mental health mean scores (Table 7.14) clearly show this predictive relationship. That is, the higher percentage of Type As in the environment, the lower the overall mental well being. Table 7.11A also shows that accident victims are significantly more likely to be Type A (mean score .455, compared to accident free individuals with a score of .340). Type A coronary-prone behaviour is therefore an important factor to consider in the offshore environment; it features as the number one predictor of all mental health sub-scale scores, except phobic anxiety (see Table 7.24). However, it must be remembered that it is the interactive nature of the three independent variables that should be considered and not Type A behaviour in isolation.

It is not surprising to find that "relationships at work and at home" feature as a predictor of overall mental health. Life and work offshore is characterised by constant company over long periods of time and it seems logical that a deterioration in working relationships may be a source of distress and subsequently reduced mental well being for some individuals. The disruption to social and community life onshore, the constant transition from one environment to the other, and over-spill of problems from one area of life to another are equally likely to be sources of stress and ultimately reduced mental well being, until finally one condition exacerbates the other. Therefore, the importance of social support in one or both areas of home or work cannot be underestimated and attention to team/group development and improved on-site management of work crews are factors for consideration.

The third predictor of mental health is the psychosocial and occupational stressor Factor 5, titled "living in the environment". This refers to the stress associated with lack of privacy, the need to share living and sleeping accommodation, and the disturbances that result from this mode of living. An individual working in the environment with the same people over long hours, and for many days at a time, also has this "constant company" burden when work is over. There is no escape from a poor working relationship, and ultimately deterioration in one area of life offshore (living or working) may aggravate the other. Conversely, "good" relationships in one area of life may help to overcome problems in another, thus acting as a "buffer" or a form of social support.

Free floating anxiety

The predictors of free-floating anxiety (accounting for 35% of the variance, Table 7.24) are the same as for overall mental well being, except that the "marital status" of being divorced, separated or widowed, is predictive of high levels of free-floating anxiety (6% of the total sample).

Obsessionality

In addition to Type A behaviour, the stress associated with the "interface between the job and the family" (Factor 7) is predictive of obsessionality (accounting for 21% of the variance, Table 7.24). The stress of the ever present issues of "leaving a wife or partner to cope and make decisions", feeling threatened by a wife or partner's independence and attitude to offshore working and the ultimate risk of partnership breakdown are all contributory to this deleterious pattern of behaviour. The high percentage (19%) of individuals offshore with obsessionality scores in the range of psycho-neurotic out-patients make this an issue which warrants further attention.

Depression

Predictors of depression (29% of the variance, Table 7.24) include Type A behaviour, the "relationships" stressor factor in the main, and the demographic variables of "level of education", "age" and "marital status" contribute a small, but significant amount to the total variance. Thus the lower the educational qualifications, the more likely higher levels of depression will be observed. Also, supporting other research findings, (Crown & Crisp, 1979), it is observed that levels of depression are likely to increase with age and peaking at around 50–54 years. Again the marital status of being widowed, divorced or separated, is a predictor of higher levels of depression.

Phobic anxiety

The stressor Factor 5 "living in the environment", and the demographic variable "number of years offshore" are not surprisingly predictive of phobic anxiety (although these are significant they are not very strong predictors, accounting for only 5% of the variance). It does however make sense intuitively that phobias related to crowds and enclosed spaces and heights may develop in this environment over time. It is an issue that requires further investigation, especially as 18.5% of the total sample have scores in the range of psycho-neurotic out-patients.

Somatic anxiety

Again the factors of Type A behaviour, and "relationships at work and at home" emerged as predictors of somatic anxiety, and account for 14% of the variance (Table 7.24). Worry or concern over poor relationships may result in disruption to sleep patterns and lead to tiredness, exhaustion and appetite loss which would ultimately effect one's ability to cope with difficult relationships at work or at home, thus setting up a vicious downward spiral. As already observed, the occupational group suffer less somatic anxiety than their onshore counterparts and is perhaps due to a "catch-up" effect during the long periods of time off.

Hysteria

Predictors of hysteria include Type A behaviour (accounting for 12% of the variance), stressor Factor 3, "factors intrinsic to the job", number of children (inversely correlated) and size of installation (inversely correlated). Thus the "no child" status is predictive of hysteria levels. As already observed, this occupational group have high "H" scores (5.1), which is likely to be a measure of sociability, youth and extraversion (Crisp *et al.*, 1978). In fact, 41% of this relatively young population do not have any children, even though 70% are either married or living with a partner. Also the smaller the offshore installation, the higher the level of "hysteria" is likely to be observed. It may be that the "extravert" or "social type" prefers the smaller working unit (less than 100 personnel) where it is possible to get to know people and be known, rather than the larger, more impersonal installations with 300 or 400 people working at any one time.

Stepwise multiple regression — job dissatisfaction

As can be seen from Table 7.23, the factor that predicted a very high percentage of the variance (29%) was again the stressor factor "relationships at work and at home". "Uncertainty in the work environment" (Factor 4), "factors intrinsic to the job" (Factor 3) and the demographic variable "number of children", also accounted for a significant, but only incremental amount of the variance.

Although three out of the top twelve stressors (Table 7.3) related in some way to the finances of the offshore worker, it was suggested (Section 8.2) that the underlying issues should be considered in addition to the more tangible resolution of these sources of stress. This referred to the situation of "comparison" among individuals in the offshore environment and the resulting dissatisfaction and frustration that this causes. It is a situation that results in the deterioration of relationships. Thus, it is seen that ultimately the main predictor of job dissatisfaction is due to the quality of relationships at work, and by interactive processes, the quality of relationships at home. More effective site management, team/crew building and development and attention to the more tangible issues of differentials are necessary to overcome this problem of job dissatisfaction.

The second predictor of job dissatisfaction was the stressor factor number four, "the uncertainty element of the work environment". Uncertainty, or the unknown, is related to the perceived degree of control over one's environment. Having to deal with "uncertainty" is therefore likely to be a source of stress for some individuals. For example, the stress of "inadequate specific training for the offshore environment", working with inadequately trained people, and mixing and working with people from different countries, is related to this element of the unknown and uncertainty, which may result in dissatisfaction with one's job.

"Factors intrinsic to job" (Factor 3) also emerged as a small, but significant predictor of job dissatisfaction. This relates to the specific types of shift patterns (the least commom patterns, see Appendix VB) and actual working conditions, for example, exposure to cold, heat, noise and vibration. These unsatisfactory conditions result in job dissatisfaction generally and may ultimately lead to an increased vulnerability to accidents.

The final predictor is the demographic variable of "number of children". It is suggested that the financial responsibility of children, the need to keep one's job in these times of high unemployment and the stress associated in being separated from one's children, are perhaps the underlying sources of this predictor. Thus, the individual stays because he perceives no alternative (real or apparent) but is dissatisfied because he is pressured into the environment. It is interesting to observe that this factor also featured as a predictor of mental health, contributing to 1% of the variance, but not reaching significance.

Calculation of the percentage of individuals without children, by installation type and sector, was found to be positively related to mean job satisfaction scores (Tables 7.2, 7.12). Thus the Dutch production personnel, with job satisfaction scores comparably favourable to the normative data, have the highest percentage of individuals without children (43% of the Dutch production sample, compared to 38% of the U.K. production group, who have significantly lower levels of job satisfaction, Table 7.12). It is also likely that age of children is important, but sample sizes are too small to make any comparisons in this study.

9 Conclusions, recommendations and future research

JOB SATISFACTION

With the exception of the Dutch production employees, compared to onshore workers, this occupational group are much less satisfied at work. Although the "uncertainty" element and certain "factors intrinsic to the job" (for example, unpleasant working conditions due to cold, vibration and noise, see Appendix VB) are predictive of job dissatisfaction, it is clear that the main contributor to job satisfaction is the quality of "relationships at work", and by nature of interactive processes "relationships at home". This is not surprising in that life and work offshore is characterised by forced contact over long periods of time, and so it would seem logical that a deterioration in working relationships would be a source of job dissatisfaction. Deterioration in working relationships as a result of perceived unfair differentials leads to dissatisfaction, frustration and lack of self esteem. Comparison with one's neighbours and peers is a basic fact of human nature.

"The quest for community will not be denied, for it springs from some of the powerful needs of human nature — need for a clear sense of cultural purpose, membership, status and continuity. Without these, no amount of mere material welfare will serve to arrest the developing sense of alienation in our society."

Robert A. Nisbet, 1962

Constant company, crowded accommodation and difficult working conditions all serve to aggravate poor interpersonal relationships offshore. It should be pointed out that, in general, the production platforms in the southern sector of the North Sea are much smaller in terms of numbers of people offshore than in the upper, northern sectors, and this might, in part, explain the differences observed in levels of job satisfation.

Neither is it surprising that the demographic variable "number of children" emerges as a predictor of job dissatisfaction. The stress associated with being separated from one's children, financial responsibility and the need to keep one's job in times of high unemployment in order to maintain a large family, are perhaps the underlying issues associated with this relationship. Job dissatisfaction ultimately leads to a reduced mental well being, physiological ill health and possible increased vulnerability to accidents. In organisational terms it results in poor performance and reduced productivity.

MENTAL HEALTH

Although overall mental well being compares favourably with onshore industrial males and general practice male groups (Crown & Crisp, 1979), with the exception of the Dutch production platform workers, levels of anxiety are significantly higher than comparable population norms. However, a disturbingly high proportion of offshore workers falls within the psycho-neurotic outpatients norms category on the sub-scales of obsessionality and phobic anxiety.

Crown & Crisp (1966) suggest that obsessionality means meticulousness, adherence to routine, punctuality, dislike of sudden change, a need to control the environment, tendency to overcheck, and a dislike of dirt. Although some of these qualities would appear to be important to maintain good housekeeping and a safe environment, it may be that the environment is eliciting and reinforcing these behaviours in an over-zealous manner, to the extent, that these over-obsessional individuals suffer a reduced mental well-being, which also has consequences for this behaviour in the home environment. This may also explain the significantly high free floating anxiety scores.

The large percentage of individuals with excessively high phobic anxiety scores is cause for concern in that the C.C.E.I. investigates phobias such as "fear of enclosed spaces", "heights" and "crowds". All issues that would be relevant to living and working conditions in the offshore environment. Individuals who suffer from these phobias, but stay in the environment because no suitable onshore work is available, may be more vulnerable to an accident because of this reduced mental well-being, and are thus a potential danger to themselves and others.

The significantly lower somatic anxiety scores (mean score = 2.5) than general male population scores (mean score = 4.3) is however encouraging. Despite working long hours over a long period of time, the offshore worker appears to be less tired and exhausted than his onshore counterpart, perhaps the result of the long periods of time off, when "catch-up" may be possible.

The main predictor of reduced mental well-being is the personality characteristic Type A "coronary-prone behaviour". However, it is not known whether this type of person is attracted to the industry and environment, or whether the environment is eliciting and reinforcing the behaviour.

The factor of "relationships" which features as the main predictor of job satisfaction, also emerges as a significant predictor of overall mental well-being, and many of the sub-scale measures (free floating anxiety, depression, and somatic anxiety). The problems associated with "poor working relationships", "disruption to home and social life", "the constant transition from one environment to another", and the "overspill of problems from one area of life to another", are likely to be sources of stress which ultimately reduce mental well-being for the offshore worker. The necessity of "sharing living/sleeping accommodation", the subsequent "disturbance from other people" and "lack of privacy", all serve to aggravate the situation in the living environment offshore. Stress associated with "being separated from one's partner", "the frequent partings and reunions" and the "burden of responsibility of relationships" may also adversely interact and affect the mental well-being of offshore workers.

Bhagat (1983) suggests that life strains increase the frequency of anxiety and depressive symptoms and this will affect job performance and subsequent job satisfaction. In organisational terms the consequences are of decreased productivity. Increased vulnerability to accidents is yet another consequence, with significant costs involved both for the individual and the organisation. As Schmidt (1985) states, "safe employees are well adjusted people". Part of the remedy here is one of more intense screening and selection of individuals into the industry. However, research is needed to establish whether the environment is eliciting and reinforcing deleterious behaviours, or if a certain type of individual is attracted to this way of life.

PERSONALITY CHARACTERISTICS

In this study two aspects of personality were analysed, coronary-prone Type-A behaviour, and locus of control, which is the degree of control perceived by the individual.

Type A coronary prone behaviour

Irrespective of whether Type A behaviour is viewed as a stable, enduring trait (Jenkins, 1976) or a style of behaviour and a habitual response to a stress stimulus (McMichael, 1978), it is an important moderator variable in the response to a stressor in the environment. As Caplan (1971) suggests "Type A individuals are more prone to perceive stress in an exaggerated fashion". Individuals offshore identified as Type As are observed to be much less satisfied with their job and suffer a greatly reduced level of overall mental well-being than their Type B counterparts. The significance and importance of this is apparent when one observes the accident record data. Self selection over time may be in operation, but this is costly in terms of turnover rates, training, accidents and disruption to stable work crews and again, more attention to selection methods, might be of benefit. However, the prevalence of Type Bs in the Dutch sector may be due to an inherent characteristic of that particular national group, and so it is necessary to observe a U.K. drilling group of individuals before any firm conclusions can be made. Future research into Type A behaviour should ideally be based on a prospective, not a retrospective, design and include objective physiological measures as well as self report subjective ratings. In the long term, there is also a need to screen employees and examine health records to investigate risk levels and incidence of coronary heart disease among this occupational group.

Locus of control

The personality characteristic of locus of control as a moderator of stress in the environment was also examined. In general, internally orientated individuals will cope more successfully with a stress situation than an "external" because of the belief that they are in control of the situation, and are not the victims of fate or luck. However, in a situation where they have little or no control, for example noise or vibration in the environment, they suffer more anxiety and display a greater reduction in performance than externals who do not have any control expectation. The predominance of "externals" in some areas of the environment offshore is not surprising, in that, "unpleasant working conditions due to noise", was rated in the stress range 3–5 by 60% of the respondents; and "disturbance due to noise from other people in the living accommodation" was rated in the 3–5 range by 41% of the sample. Rotter (1966) suggests that "internals" will suffer more in a noisy situation, over which they have no control, and it would follow, therefore, that there may be some self-selection operating, with "externals" opting for offshore work. Significantly more "externals" were found in the U.K. production area, and this is also the group of employees with the lowest rate of accidents. However, observation of a U.K. drilling sample is needed, objective and subjective reports of noise across various occupations with a larger survey sample generally, before any firm conclusions can be made.

ACCIDENTS

It is not known whether the observed behaviour (i.e. less job satisfaction, reduced mental well-being, depression and obsessional behaviour) of accident victims, versus those who are accident free, is the outcome of the incident or was the initial cause (either in whole or in part). However, it is also interesting to note that these accident victims are also likely to be Type As, as opposed to "accident free" Type Bs. The high percentage of Type As reporting "accident involvement leading to injury" is disturbing, and may be a direct consequence of the Type A behaviour of "haste and time urgency" (Haynes, 1978), or the fact that the job itself elicits Type A behaviour, and subsequent vulnerability to accidents. There may be some relationship with this Type A behaviour and the high scores obtained on the "H" sub scale measure of mental health. Although labelled "hysteria" it is suggested that it is more likely to be a measure of sociability and extraversion. It is therefore suggested that this factor of extraversion be examined more closely in future research. Regardless of explanation, Type A behaviour seems to be a very important predictor of offshore accidents, and must, therefore, be investigated further.

SAFETY

Although the factor of safety in the offshore environment (number 6, Appendix VB) did not emerge as a predictor of job satisfaction, or mental well-being, there are some points worthy of mention.

Although Bohemier (1985) suggests it is human nature not to think about danger, 39% of the respondents acknowledge the stress of working in a hazardous environment, by rating it in the 3–5 stress range. However a certain amount of resentment exists that safety offshore is obsessional. This is perhaps a reaction to a situation where the individual is unable to repress fears or concern about safety because of the constant reminder of the reality of the environment, or it may be that the competent, trained employee does not regard the environment as a danger. Despite these attitudes, the risk to personal safety offshore was identified as a source of stress in the environment.

The major concern for a large percentage of personnel was the stress associated with long periods of intense concentration, keeping up with changes and new equipment, and the fear of making a mistake. Although praise of specific courses regarding safety offshore is evident, the criticism is often that they are untimely. The use of simulators in training might be a useful consideration, and although expensive, the costs should be evaluated in terms of costs of accidents offshore. Some degree of success is reported in the United States with crane operation simulators (*Offshore*, August 1985).

Safety offshore must not be seen only to pay lip-service, nor to be a matter of politics. Use of role play techniques may be applied as a successful (active versus passive) method of attitude change towards more positive and safer ways of working. It is recognised as more beneficial than lectures, debate and poster campaigns. Also, more attention should be paid to first aid training, generally to overcome the stress related to feelings of inadequacy when an accident occurs. Finally, it is important that detailed reports of all accidents and incidents, however minor, are kept if vulnerability to accidents is to be seriously studied, and the significant predictors of accidents identified.

FURTHER RECOMMENDATIONS

The suggestion of an improved and more comprehensive selection and assessment process has already been put forward as a means of overcoming some of the problems related to personnel offshore. Identification of unsuitable behavioural and personality characteristics may be important. Selection methods can also be used to overcome specific problems, for example, if travel from the home base is a source of stress, or the heterogeneous population offshore is a significant source of stress. However, a second major recommendation refers to the improvement of man-management offshore and the need to introduce team/crew building and development as vital steps towards improving interpersonal relationships, the underlying cause of many sources of psychosocial and occupational stress in the environment.

Good team working has already been identified as the most important factor for successful coping with life offshore (Livy & Vant, 1979) and is linked to the benefits of social support from one's colleagues. This would seem to be an important point especially as a source of stress is identified as "not having someone to talk over problems with". A better solution might be to incorporate "counselling" into the duties of an offshore employee. Kabanoff (1980) suggests that social support works in three ways: "Spillover", where the events of one environment affect the other. This interactive feature is important in an environment where relationships at work and at home are identified as the most significant source of stress. Secondly, social support may act as compensatory, where one element of the environment compensates for something lacking in another. Finally, where the environments are said to be independent and the individual is able to compartmentalise the various components of his life.

Improved man-management is part of successful team building in overcoming problems of lack of co-operation and reducing the apparent gulf between groups offshore (for example, operator and contractor personnel; although it may be necessary to have an authority figure offshore representing the contractors, to overcome some of these problems). However, more basic issues of management also require attention and will help to alleviate some of the sources of stress offshore. These include improved time management, especially with crew change arrangements. By nature of the job, some things cannot be radically changed, but should be examined to find ways of minimising stress. For example, the improved man-management practice of maintaining stability in work crews where possible.

The results of this study also have implications for the design of offshore installations, with more attention paid to living accommodation. For example, single, as opposed to shared, and thereby reducing the stress associated with lack of privacy, and constant, forced contact with other people.

The results of this study are drawn from the responses of individuals located on a total of thirty-one drilling rigs and production platforms in the U.K. and Dutch sectors of the North Sea. Views are expressed of forty-four different offshore occupations. It is thus a very general and wide impression of life and working conditions offshore but which may serve to reduce criticism normally levied at the use of a pre-designed job stressor questionnaire in respect of the limited population on which it was based, and where certain stressors may be rejected and the importance of others distorted (Crump *et al.*, 1980). However, the use of traditional Likert-type rating scales does not allow one to observe both the pressure of stressors in the environment, and the fact that they may also be a source of satisfaction to the individual (Glowinkowski & Cooper, 1985). There is a need to consider to what extent a certain degree of stress is beneficial to the individual (Bernard, 1968).

Future research should consider these issues and may perhaps successfully employ the use of repertory grid techniques to focus on particular groups in specific areas of the offshore environment.

This study attempts to add to our minimal knowledge of stress among blue-collar workers, but it is only the first step towards an understanding of psychosocial and occupational stress in the offshore oil and gas extraction industries in the Dutch and United Kingdom controlled sector of the North Sea. As Selye (1956) suggests, an understanding of the mechanisms of stress can guide one's actions throughout life. He states,

"... it is not to see something first, but to establish solid connections between the previously known and the hitherto unknown that constitutes the essence of scientific discovery". This is just a beginning.

APPENDIX I

Glossary of terms*

A.P.I. American Petroleum Institute. An association incorporated in the U.S.A. having as its object the study of the arts and sciences connected with the petroleum industry in all its branches and the fostering of foreign and domestic trade in American petroleum products.

Block Subdivision of sea area for purpose of licensing to a company or companies for exploration/production rights. A U.K. block is approximately 200–250 sq. km., and is defined by lines of latitude at ten minute intervals and lines of longitude at twelve minute intervals, giving thirty blocks in each 1 degree by 1 degree major division or quadrant. The Norwegian and Dutch blocks are larger, the former varying from 500 to 570 sq. km. and the latter from 390 to 420 sq. km.

Blow-out An escape of oil or gas (usually accidental) from a well during the drilling stage.

Casing Steel lining used to prevent caving of the sides of a well, to exclude unwanted fluids, and to provide means for the control of well pressures and oil and gas production.

Christmas Tree Assembly of valves and fittings located at the head of a well to control the flow of oil and gas.

Circulating Fluid Liquid, air, or gas "circulated" in a bore-hole during rotary drilling operations.

Concession The right to drill for oil or gas on a block obtained under licence from the State.

Continental Shelf The shallow, submerged platform, bordering and marking the structural edge of the continent. The use of the term "shelf" is reserved for the sea-bed of a depth of 200 metres and less.

Derrick The steel structure, used to support the drill pipe and other equipment which has to be raised or lowered during well-drilling operations.

Derrick Barge A crane barge used in the offshore construction industry, suitable for working in rough seas. These barges are equipped with cranes of varying capabilities up to 3,000 tons.

*Source: *Offshore Oil and Gas Yearbook 1983/84. U.K. and Continental Europe.* Based on the publication *"The Oil and Gas Industry: A Glossary of Terms"*, produced by the Bank of Scotland Information Service.

162

Development Wells Wells which are drilled for the purpose of producing oil and/or gas. They are drilled within the productive area defined by appraisal and stepout wells after an oil or gas accumulation has proved sufficiently large for exploitation.

Discovery Well A successful exploration well.

Doghouse A shelter on the drilling floor for the use of rig hands and others.

Downtime The time during which a drilling rig or any other item of equipment (for instance a lay barge) is not able to operate owing to adverse weather conditions or other factors.

Drill Pipe Steel pipe used for carrying and rotating the drilling tools in a well and for permitting the circulation of drilling fluid.

Drilling It may take 60 days to sink an exploratory well 3km into the bed of the North Sea. As it goes down, steel tubes, decreasing in diameter from 760 mm to 180 mm are cemented in at different depths to line the hole — up to 500 tons of steel may be built in as a consumable in this way whether the well is successful or not, and in all, with drilling mud, cement and other consumables up to 3,000 tons of material will be used. Drilling mud is pumped down the centre of the drill pipe to cool the bit, wash chippings to the surface and hold back the high oil pressure released when the caprock is penetrated. One of the methods of damping down a well which has gone out of control is to pump high density barytes base mud down the well. Rotational drive only is provided for the drill pipe; its own weight is enough to keep the bit in contact with rock.

Drilling Fluid (mud) Fluid, commonly consisting of clay suspended in water, used in drilling wells. It is pumped down through the drill-string to the bottom of the bore-hole, whence it rises to the surface through the space between drill-string and bore-hole wall.

Drilling Platform Structure used in offshore drilling to support the drilling rig and to house other facilities and stores. A fixed platform, used for development drilling, rests on piles driven into the sea bed or is kept in position by its own weight. The former usually constructed from steel, the latter is known as a gravity platform and can be either concrete, or steel and concrete "hybrid". Both these types of platforms may be so designed and sited as to permit the drilling of a number of wells by using directional drilling. Mobile platforms, usually referred to as mobile rigs and used for explatory drilling, are of several kinds. Three common kinds are: 1. Drill ships: free-floating "ship-shaped" vessels which are kept in position by multiple anchors or by dynamic positioning. 2. Jack-up platforms with retractable legs, which can be lowered to the sea bed and then enable the body (hull) of the platform to be raised to a safe distance above the sea's surface. 3. Semi-submersible, with pontoons, or floats which are submerged to give the platform stability while floating, and are suitably anchored or dynamically positioned.

Drilling Rig The complete machinery and structures required for drilling a well.

Term also commonly used to describe mobile platforms used for exploratory drilling offshore.

Exploitation The development or drilling-up and producing phase of an oilfield, following the exploration phase.

Exploration The phase in which a possible oil region is being investigated either by geological or geophysical surveys or by exploratory drilling. Successful exploration is followed by exploitation.

I.P. Institute of Petroleum: the industry-sponsored organisation in Great Britain primarily responsible for the advancement of the study of petroleum and its allied products in all their aspects. It is the recognised British standardisation authority for methods of testing petroleum products.

Jacket The term used to describe the support structure (basically the legs), of a steel production platform. This structure is fixed to the sea-bed by piling and then the superstructure consisting of all the equipment modules is mounted on it.

Kelly Hollow, 40 foot long, square or hexagonal pipe attached to the top of the drill-string and turned by the rotary table during drilling. It is used to transmit the torque or twisting movement from the rotary machinery to the drill-string and thus to the bit.

Killing a Well Stopping the flow from a well by filling the wellbore with drilling mud of suitable density.

Lay Barge Specialised barge used for laying submarine pipelines. It may be designed on the semi-submersible principle.

Log A detailed drilling record which gives the nature, thickness, content, etc., of the formations encountered in a well.

Mud See drilling fluid.

O.P.E.C. (and O.A.P.E.C.) The Organisation of Petroleum Exporting Countries, consisting of Algeria, Ecuador, Gabon, Indonesia, Iran, Iraq, Kuwait, Libya, Nigeria, Qatar, Saudi Arabia, United Arab Emirates and Venezuela. The Organisation was formed in 1960 with the aim of co-ordinating its members' policies on price, production rates and taxation, O.A.P.E.C. is the Organisation of Arab Petroleum Exporting Countries.

Operating Company or Operator The company in a consortium which carries out the drilling and subsequent production, if a proven commercial field is found, on blocks which are held by consortia of several companies.

Pay Zone The reservoir rock in which oil and gas are found in exploitable quantities.

Petroleum Mineral oil, normally a liquid mixture consisting essentially of many different hydrocarbons, occurring naturally and having a wide range of colours from yellow to black, and characteristic odours. It is the raw material from which gasoline, kerosine, lubricating oil, fuel oil, paraffin wax, bitumen and other products are obtained. In modern technical usage the term includes gaseous and solid as well as liquid hydrocarbons.

Recovery Techniques There are essentially three methods of oil recovery, namely primary involving the use of natural pressures in the reservoir, secondary involving water or gas injection, and tertiary involving the use of steam, fire, chemicals, fracturing etc. Recovery phases usually overlap.

Rig See drilling rig.

Rotary Table Chain or gear-driven circular unit, mounted in the derrick floor which rotates the drill pipe and bit.

Roughneck Sometimes called a floorman. These members of the rig crew set the slips to hold the drill pipe, handle the tongs or elevators and generally handle the equipment around the rig floor.

Round Trip The complete process of pulling out and running in the drill-string, for instance to replace a worn bit.

Roustabout General labourer employed on the rig, whose job it is to unload equipment from the supply boats, and generally to maintain the rig area.

Semi-Submersible See drilling platforms.

Spud in (or Spudding) To commence drilling operations by "making a hole".

Standby Vessel A smallish vessel, often a converted trawler, chartered for the sole purpose of remaining on location as near as possible to the rig, in case of accidents. It should not be confused with a supply or service vessel, which is used to ferry supplies to the rig and is usually a larger, much more versatile vessel, often capable of handling the huge anchors used for rigs, and of towing rigs, and having considerable open deck and cargo space for carrying bulk supplies such as drill pipe, drilling cement, etc.

Tension Leg Platform A floating steel or concrete platform which is anchored to the sea bed by adjustable cables. The cables keep the platform on station, tension in the cables being maintained by the platform's buoyancy.

Toolpusher Drilling supervisor, in other words, the foreman in charge of the operation of the rig.

Tour A drilling shift, usually of twelve hours.

Wildcat Well drilled in search of a new oil or gas accumulation — an exploration well.

Workover Re-entry into a completed well for modification or repair work.

W.O.W. Waiting on Weather; usually applied to mobile offshore drilling plat-forms but can also refer to other offshore operations.

Interview schedule

To highlight the problems and pressures associated with employment on offshore oil/gas installations.

Organisational Demands:

A   Role demands; the job; reasons for job choice; satisfaction — likes/dislikes; scope; responsibilities — people/things (too little, too much) role conflict; ambiguity; clarity; managing people (discipline/sacking); support. Status. Performance evaluation.

Ai   Career — development; life stage; security/the future — ambition; promotion (over/under) recruitment; training (adequate); transfers; adequacy of pay/bonus/pensions. Fulfilment; creativity.

Aii Organisation and climate; politics; participation; restrictions on behaviour — freedom to act — negotiate; beliefs (same/different) conflict of loyalty; any structural/procedural changes which would benefit you?

B   Task Demand: physical factors intrinsic to job — hours worked; varieties of shifts; regularity/inconvenience; clarity of task; exploitation of knowledge; overload/underload; adequate supervision; contribution to task — individual or shared outcomes; keeping up with new equipment/technology; time pressure/able to keep-up — meet deadlines; admin/paper work; mistakes —errors; risk of accidents/safety (personal/rig); travel to and from job; weather/climate.

C   Physical Demands: environmental conditions — heat/cold — noise crowding/sharing — privacy; communication with outside world; equipment used; adequacy of medical facilities; male dominated environment; services — food etc. Confinement/restriction. Relaxation facilities/ adequate.

D   Interpersonal Demands; relationships at work with boss/peers/subordinates — nature of: good/bad — trust — social support; levels of communication; attitudes of others; cliques; reliance on others (all pull weight); closeness of living conditions. Co-operation/competition. Abrasive personalities/violence. Meeting and working with a variety of people. Ethnicity.

Extraorganisational Demands:

E   Social Responsibilities: home/work interface — social/cultural background factors; social life; community ties/integration into the community; relocation related problems; pace of life.

F   Marriage/Dependent Relationships: individual private life worlds; spouse/children/dependents — attitudes to your work; demands of work on my relationships; disruption of home life; ability of wife to cope; independence of wife etc. — associated problems of adjustment while on leave; separation/divorce; relocation of family.

G   Self-Imposed Responsibilities: Expectations; aspirations; commitment; control; Strengths/Weakness important to ability to cope/perform the job; perceived power/influence. Self esteem.

H   Other comments.

I   Interview remarks.

. . . .

Job Title: Age:
Length of Service with D:
Length of time on this location:
Previous assignments:

Marital status:
No. of children: Ages:
Other dependants:

Educational Qualifications:

Professional Qualifications:

Career History (previous to D):

Religion:

Accidents: type   lost time

Medical: Doctor   Hospital   Medication
                      Health problems:

                      Do you smoke: no:
                      Do you drink Alcohol:
                      Do you take regular exercise: type/frequency

The survey questionnaire

Dear Sir,

We hope by now that you have received your Company's Newsletter describing the project we are working on, "Stress in the Oil Industry". Just to remind you, we are trying to identify the source of stressors for personnel working in the offshore oil and gas industry.

.... has acknowledged the importance of this research by offering us its full support and co-operation. The first stage of the project is already complete, and we have successfully carried out interviews with many of your colleagues in Holland and Aberdeen. This questionnaire, stage two of the project, has been prepared from the interviews; it also includes measures of job satisfaction, health, health behaviours and personality.

Please take a little of your time to fill out this booklet and post it back to us in the pre-paid, addressed envelope. We hope you will not find it too much of a burden because the success of this stage depends on your help. It is your opportunity to tell us about living and working on offshore drilling rigs and production platforms. We therefore urge you to take part and return this to us in Manchester as quickly as possible.

It is not necessary to identify yourself, so any information you give will be both anonymous and confidential.

The results of this project will be presented to .... They will be published and made available to anyone interested. Meanwhile, your Newsletter will keep you informed about the progress of the project.

We would like to take this opportunity to thank you for your contribution, time and co-operation,

Yours faithfully,

Explanations

PLEASE READ THIS INFORMATION PAGE BEFORE YOU START TO
COMPLETE THE QUESTIONNAIRE

THIS BOOKLET

In this booklet you will find an array of questionnaires. They are mainly
checklists and each has its own set of instructions. Please read each set of
instructions before starting to complete each checklist.

HOW TO ANSWER

For many of the questions please ring the number opposite your answer. If you
make a mistake and ring the wrong number, cross it out and ring the correct
number. For example,

$$\begin{array}{ll} \text{The year is 1983} & 1 \\ 1984 & \cancel{2} \\ 1985 & \circledR \end{array}$$

For other questions you simply write in your answer or complete as scheduled. If
you are required to insert a number, please enter only one digit into each box
provided.

We can not be present when you complete this booklet, and so must depend on
you to complete all questionnaires under "scientific conditions". The following
points may help you.

1.   Try and give your first and natural answer. This is best achieved by
       working quickly, but be as honest and accurate as you can be.
2.   The questionnaires are to be completed by you and no one else.
3.   The information must be given by you in private. Remember, we will keep
       all the data confidential, so must you.
4.   Although some individual questions might seem unusual, remember that
       we will be looking at groups of items, so please answer all questions.
5.   Please remember the overall project objectives. We are trying to identify
       stressors for those people working in the offshore oil and gas industries.
6.   Please ignore the right hand column "FOR OFFICE USE ONLY". It is our
       own numbering system.
7.   THIS IS A CONFIDENTIAL SURVEY. *ALL INDIVIDUAL DATA WILL
       REMAIN MEDICALLY IN CONFIDENCE* AND WILL NOT BE DIVULGED
       TO ANY EXTERNAL BODY.

After you have read this page, please read the next page for further explanations.

SECTION A

For the purpose of analysis only, please answer the following questions about yourself. Your answers will remain *anonymous and strictly confidential*. This information is *crucial* to the study.

Answer the following questions by *circling* eg. ②, the most appropriate response unless otherwise instructed.

1. What is your job title? _____

2. Would you describe your job as:

Unskilled	1
Semi Skilled	2
Skilled	3

3. Are you working on a

Drilling rig	1
Production platform	2

4. The name of the rig or platform _____

5. How many people on this rig/platform on average?   approximately _____

6. Identify your present work pattern

7 days on — 7 days off only days	1
7 days on — 7 days off alternate weeks of days and nights	2
14 days on — 14 days off only days	3
14 days on — 14 days off a mix of day and night shift	4
other — please specify _____	5

7. How many years have you worked in the offshore oil/gas industry   _____ years

8. Have you worked on both drilling and production operations?

Yes	1
No	2

9. How many years have you been with this present Company _____

10.   What was the last job you had before going to
      work offshore?
         Job Title ———————————————
         Type of Company/Factory ——————————
         For how many years? ——————————

OFFICE USE ONLY

11.   What is your age?   12.   Are you:

Under 25	1	Married	1
26–30	2	Remarried - once	2
31–35	3	- twice	3
36–40	4	Living together	4
41–50	5	Single	5
51–60	6	Divorced	6
Over 60	7	Separated	7
		Widower	8

13.   Number of Children: 14.   Age of Children:

None	1	Not applicable	1
One	2	All pre-school age	2
Two	3	Pre-school and	
Three	4	school age	3
Four or more	5	All school age	4
		School age and post	
		school age	5
		All post school age	6

15.   What is the highest educational qualification, if any,
      that you have attained?

None	1
GCE 'O' Level/CSE	2
'A' Level/Ordinary National Diploma	3
Higher National Diploma or equivalent	4
University Degree	5
MA/MSc	6
PhD	7
Other (please specify)	8

16.   Please specify any technical qualifications you have;
      including apprenticeships, certificates and diplomas

      ————————————————————————————
      ————————————————————————————
      ————————————————————————————
      ————————————————————————————

17.   Do you supervise other people
         Yes   1
         No   2

18.   How many people do you supervise? _____

SECTION B

Could you please circle the number that best reflects the degree to which the particular statement is a source of stress in your life as an offshore worker in the oil/gas industry. The word "stress" should be interpreted in a wide sense, that is, worry, tension, anxiety, anger or perhaps just mild irritation.

Only when a statement/situation *does not apply to you,* circle NA for Not Applicable, e.g. circle NA for 'sharing sleeping accommodation', if you sleep alone in a cabin.

There are no right or wrong answers. Try to give your first and natural answer, this is easiest to do if you work quickly and without time spent pondering.

Codes   5 = a source of extreme stress
         3 = a source of moderate stress
         1 = no stress at all

Therefore if *"the routine nature of my job"* is a slight pressure for you, you would circle 2 e.g.

	No Stress			High Stress	
the routine nature of my job	1 ② 3	4	5	NA

or, if *"lack of privacy"* is a very difficult problem for you, then you might circle 4, or 5, depending on how strongly you feel about the issue.

	No Stress			High Stress	
1 Working in a hazardous/ dangerous environment	1 2 3	4	5	NA
2 I don't feel enough is done towards personal safety	1 2 3	4	5	NA
3 The routine nature of my job	1 2 3	4	5	NA
4 Sometimes I feel I don't have time to do the job properly	1 2 3	4	5	NA

		No Stress				High Stress		OFFICE USE ONLY
5	The variety and uncertainty in my job	1	2	3	4	5	NA	
6	Long periods of intense concentration	1	2	3	4	5	NA	
7	Working long hours	1	2	3	4	5	NA	
8	Boredom — not enough to do	1	2	3	4	5	NA	
9	Working 7 days on/off — days	1	2	3	4	5	NA	
10	Working 7 days on/off — alternate weeks days & nights	1	2	3	4	5	NA	
11	Working 14 days on/off	1	2	3	4	5	NA	
12	Working 14 days on/off day and night shifts	1	2	3	4	5	NA	
13	Working 28 days on/off	1	2	3	4	5	NA	
14	Last minute changes in crew relief arrangements	1	2	3	4	5	NA	
15	Keeping up with changes and new equipment	1	2	3	4	5	NA	
16	I feel that my own and others safety is at risk if I make a mistake	1	2	3	4	5	NA	
17	Travel by helicopter	1	2	3	4	5	NA	
18	The need to crew change by supply boat	1	2	3	4	5	NA	
19	Travel from home to check-in place	1	2	3	4	5	NA	
20	Staying overnight to meet early check-in time	1	2	3	4	5	NA	
21	Delay in crew change due to weather conditions	1	2	3	4	5	NA	

		No Stress					High Stress	OFFICE USE ONLY
22	Working in severe weather conditions	1	2	3	4	5	NA	
23	Unpleasant working conditions due to:-							
	(A) heat	1	2	3	4	5	NA	
	(B) cold	1	2	3	4	5	NA	
	(C) vibration	1	2	3	4	5	NA	
	(D) noise	1	2	3	4	5	NA	
24	Sharing living/sleeping accommodation	1	2	3	4	5	NA	
25	Getting insufficient sleep when I am offshore	1	2	3	4	5	NA	
26	Disturbance in living accommodation due to:	1	2	3	4	5	NA	
	(A) Noise from other people	1	2	3	4	5	NA	
	(B) Noise from machinery	1	2	3	4	5	NA	
	(C) Heat/Cold	1	2	3	4	5	NA	
	(D) Vibration	1	2	3	4	5	NA	
27	Lack of privacy	1	2	3	4	5	NA	
28	Working in an all male environment	1	2	3	4	5	NA	
29	Lacking confidence about medical facilities	1	2	3	4	5	NA	
30	Feeling inadequate when someone has an accident	1	2	3	4	5	NA	
31	Feeling restricted/ confined	1	2	3	4	5	NA	
32	Inadequate facilitiesfor physical exercise	1	2	3	4	5	NA	
33	Inadequate leisure facilities to occupy my free time	1	2	3	4	5	NA	
34	Working relationships within my work/crew team	1	2	3	4	5	NA	

		No Stress				High Stress		OFFICE USE ONLY
35	The relationship between me and my boss/ supervisor	1	2	3	4	5	NA	
36	Deterioration in working relationships after intensive periods together	1	2	3	4	5	NA	
37	The relationship between the Contractors and the Company men	1	2	3	4	5	NA	
38	Women working offshore	1	2	3	4	5	NA	
39	Working with inadequately trained people	1	2	3	4	5	NA	
40	Not getting co-operation at work	1	2	3	4	5	NA	
41	Frequent changes in my work crew/team	1	2	3	4	5	NA	
42	Mixing and working with people from different countries	1	2	3	4	5	NA	
43	Problems arising because of language/dialect difference	1	2	3	4	5	NA	
44	Having no-one to talk over problems with	1	2	3	4	5	NA	
45	Lack of job satisfaction	1	2	3	4	5	NA	
46	Inadequate instruction to do the job	1	2	3	4	5	NA	
47	No recognition for doing a good job	1	2	3	4	5	NA	
48	Having to discipline people	1	2	3	4	5	NA	
49	Lack of job security	1	2	3	4	5	NA	
50	Lack of promotion opportunity	1	2	3	4	5	NA	

		No Stress			High Stress			OFFICE USE ONLY
51	Rate of pay	1 2	3	4 5	NA			
52	Pay differentials	1 2	3	4 5	NA			
53	Lack of paid holidays	1 2	3	4 5	NA			
54	Inadequate specific training for offshore work	1 2	3	4 5	NA			
55	Having to teach others to do the job	1 2	3	4 5	NA			
56	Not being used to my full potential	1 2	3	4 5	NA			
57	Having to work with people unsuited to offshore life and work	1 2	3	4 5	NA			
58	Feeling trapped into offshore work because no suitable onshore work is available	1 2	3	4 5	NA			
59	Having to move my wife/family to meet the demands of my job	1 2	3	4 5	NA			
60	I feel it is impossible to make changes concerning my job	1 2	3	4 5	NA			
61	Fear of being branded a trouble maker	1 2	3	4 5	NA			
62	Wife/partner's attitude to me working offshore	1 2	3	4 5	NA			
63	Leaving your wife/partner to cope/make decisions	1 2	3	4 5	NA			
64	Feeling threatened by wife/partner's independence	1 2	3	4 5	NA			
65	Having a working wife	1 2	3	4 5	NA			
66	Difficulties with my children because I work offshore	1 2	3	4 5	NA			

		No Stress				High Stress	
67	Risk of marriage breakdown because I work offshore	1	2	3	4	5	NA
68	Restricted ability to contact home while I am away	1	2	3	4	5	NA
69	Problems unwinding when I return home	1	2	3	4	5	NA
70	Disruption of my social life	1	2	3	4	5	NA
71	Unable to get involved in the community at home (e.g. clubs and organisations)	1	2	3	4	5	NA
72	Feeling isolated from home and world events while I am offshore	1	2	3	4	5	NA
73	Feeling that time is passing by too quickly	1	2	3	4	5	NA
74	Difficulties concentrating on work when my mind is thinking about home	1	2	3	4	5	NA

OFFICE USE ONLY

SECTION C

1   Have you ever had any accident/personal injury while working on an offshore drilling rig or production platform?

Yes	1
No	2

2   Please describe briefly what happened:

_____

_____

3   Time of day _____

4   Which day of the hitch, e.g. 2 of 7 (i.e. the second day of a 7 day period offshore) _____

5   How much time lost .... days

6   Have you had any time off due to personal or family
      illness *in the last year*

                        Yes   1
                        No   2

7   Please describe briefly:

      _____

      _____

      _____

8   Did you visit a doctor?   9   Did you spend any time
                                       in hospital?

          Yes   1   Yes   1
          No   2   No   2

9   How much work time was lost? _____ days

10   Over the past year, which of the following best describes
      your typical drinking habits, (one drink is a single whisky,
      gin, glass of wine etc., or ½ pint/or bottle of beer) when
      you are on shore leave?
          Teetotal   1
          An occasional drink   2
          Several drinks a week, but not every day   3
          Regularly, 1 or 2 drinks a day   4
          Regularly, 3–6 drinks a day   5
          Regularly, more than 6 drinks a day   6

11   Cigarette smoking – which of the following statements is
      most true for you?
          I have never smoked regularly   1
          I have given up smoking   2
          I am currently smoking   3

12   If you are currently smoking, please circle the number
      which constitutes your average daily consumption of
      cigarettes: (If you use loose tobacco to roll your own
      cigarettes, will you indicate approximately the number of
      cigarettes that this is equivalent to)
          (A) While offshore:
              1 – 5 a day   1
              5 – 10   "   2
              10 – 15 "   3
              15 – 20 "   4

OFFICE USE ONLY

```
                 20 – 30 a day                           5
                 30 – 40    "                            6
                 40 plus a day                           7
         (B) When at home on leave:
                  1 –  5 a day                           1
                  5 – 10    "                            2
                 10 – 15    "                            3
                 15 – 20    "                            4
                 20 – 30    "                            5
                 30 – 40    "                            6
                 40 plus a day                           7
```

13   How often do you use the following measures to relax?

		never	rarely	some-times	often	always
(a)	take sleeping pills	1	2	3	4	5
(b)	use tranquilisers	1	2	3	4	5
(c)	smoke	1	2	3	4	5
(d)	have an alcoholic drink	1	2	3	4	5
(e)	drink coffee, coke or eat frequently	1	2	3	4	5
(f)	eat junk food	1	2	3	4	5
(g)	exercise	1	2	3	4	5
(h)	talk to someone you know	1	2	3	4	5
(i)	use humour	1	2	3	4	5
(j)	other _____	1	2	3	4	5
	_____	1	2	3	4	5

14   Do you take regular exercise

```
         Yes         1          Describe please, the activity
         No          2          and how frequently
```

_____

_____

_____

SECTION D   JOB SATISFACTION

Instructions: This set of items deals with various as-
                      pects of your job. We would like you to tell
                      us how satisfied or dissatisfied you feel
                      with each of these features of your pre-
                      sent job. Please use the scale below to
                      indicate your feelings.

Please remember: There are no right or wrong answers. Give your first and natural answer by working quickly, but be accurate. Remember to answer all questions.

Just indicate how satisfied or dissatisfied you are with each of the various aspects of your job by using this scale:

     1 – I'm extremely dissatisfied
     2 – I'm very dissatisfied
     3 – I'm moderately dissatisfied
     4 – I'm not sure
     5 – I'm moderately satisfied
     6 – I'm very satisfied
     7 – I'm extremely satisfied

Simply write down in the space provided the number of your answer.

1. The physical working conditions   _____
2. The freedom to choose your own
    method of working   _____
3. Your fellow workers   _____
4. The recognition you get for good work   _____
5. Your immediate boss   _____
6. The amount of responsibility you are given   _____
7. Your rate of pay   _____
8. Your opportunity to use your abilities   _____
9. Industrial relations between management and
    workers in your firm   _____
10. Your chance of promotion   _____
11. The way your firm is managed   _____
12. The attention paid to suggestions you make   _____
13. Your hours of work   _____
14. The amount of variety in your job   _____
15. Your job security   _____
16. Now, taking everything into consideration,
    how do you feel about your job as a whole?   _____

PLEASE CHECK THAT YOU HAVE ANSWERED ALL THE QUESTIONS

SECTION E

[At this point the Crown Crisp Experiential Index was used (Crown & Crisp, 1979).]

SECTION F

Instructions: Here is a list of several traits or qualities. For each one indicate whether the trait describes you very well, fairly well, somewhat, or not at all.

		Very Well	Fairly Well	Some- what	Not at all
1.	Being bossy or dominating	1	2	3	4
2.	Having a strong need to excel (be best) in most things	1	2	3	4
3.	Usually feeling pressed for time	1	2	3	4
4.	Being hard driving and competitive	1	2	3	4
5.	Eating too quickly	1	2	3	4

With regard to your work:

		Yes	No
6.	Have you often felt very pressed for time?	1	2
7.	Have you often had a feeling of dissatisfaction	1	2
8.	Has your work often stayed with you so that you think about it all day long?	1	2
9.	In general, do (did) you find work a big strain?	1	2
10.	Do you get quite upset when you have to wait for anything?	1	2

PLEASE CHECK THAT YOU HAVE ANSWERED ALL THE QUESTIONS

SECTION G

[At this point the I.E. Scale, Rotter (1966), was used.]

SECTION H

Thank you for completing this questionnaire. Please write below any other comments you wish to include, e.g. personal experiences or illustrations, that might help us to understand the life and working conditions on offshore drilling rigs and/or production platforms with regard to stress. We would also be interested to hear about any techniques, or personal characteristics that you have personally found useful for coping with the problems and pressures associated with this working/living environment.

Offshore job titles of total survey respondents

Title	Code number	Number identified
Administrator/Radio	1	1
Administrator/Radio/Medic	2	0
Medic	3	5
Radio Operator	4	10
Teacher	5	0
Utility Man	6	7
Motorman	7	5
Electrician	8	3
Instrument Technician	9	19
Tech. Clerk/Mat. Coord	10	1
Mechanic	11	3
Rig Mechanic	12	1
Prod. Operator 2	13	0
Floorman/Roughneck	14	0
Coordinator	15	1
Roustabout/Cleaner	16	0
Roustabout	17	26
Roustabout/Painter	18	1
Roustabout/Chopperboy	19	0
Roustabout/Floorman	20	0
General Assistant	21	0
Head Roustabout	22	0
Boatswain	23	1
Roustabout/Crane Operator	24	1
First Painter/Foreman	25	2
Welder	26	6
Chopperboy	27	0
Storekeeper	28	0
Assistant Derrickman	29	1
Derrickman	30	6
Crane Operator	31	9
Deck Pusher	32	1
Mud Boy	33	1
Assistant Driller	34	3

Title	Code number	Number identified
Electrical Technician	35	11
Mechanical Technician	36	23
Riggers	37	0
Scaffolders	38	2
Platers	39	1
VDU Operators/Tech Clerk	40	1
Senior Operators	41	0
Control Room	42	1
Gas Operator	43	1
DGA Operator (Gas)	44	0
Oil Operator	45	0
Power Operator	46	3
Chemists	47	3
Fire and Gas	48	0
Drilling Consultants	49	0
Blaster/Painter	50	1
Roughneck	51	10
Operator Mechanic	52	2
Painter	53	1
Roustabout/Welder	54	1
Production Operator	55	9
Fire and Gas Roustabout	56	1
Operator Technician	57	1
Production Technician	58	3
Roustabout/Utility	59	1
Crane Operator/Deck Pusher	60	1
Rig Materials Man	61	1

Descriptive statistics and Factor analysis

A. DESCRIPTIVE STATISTICS — RESPONSES TO THE PSYCHOSOCIAL AND OCCUPATIONAL STRESSOR QUESTIONNAIRE

Number	Stressor item	Mean score	Standard deviation	% of respondents scoring in 3 – 5 stress range	% of sample responding "non-applicable"
1	Lack of paid holidays	3.7	1.50	78.3	5.2
2	Rate of pay	3.2	1.58	64.8	.5
3	Pay differentials	3.2	1.61	62.2	2.1
4	Lack of job security	3.1	1.51	65.5	2.6
5	Last minute changes in crew relief arrangements	3.0	1.45	61.5	10.3
6	Working with inadequately trained people	2.9	1.29	61.4	5.2
7	Unpleasant working conditions due to noise	2.89	1.25	60.4	3.6
8	Lack of promotion opportunity	2.84	1.41	58.8	3.1
9	Not getting co-operation at work	2.83	1.29	53.5	4.6
10	Working 28 days on/off	2.74	1.52	49.1	70.6
11	Not being used to my full potential	2.71	1.40	53.4	1.5
12	Delay in crew change due to weather conditions	2.69	1.36	49.7	1.5
13	Feeling that time is passing by too quickly	2.66	1.41	51.6	1.0
14	Inadequate leisure facilities to occupy my free time	2.57	1.35	49.2	1.5
15	Having to work with people unsuited to offshore life and work	2.54	1.38	50.0	3.1
16	No recognition for doing a good job	2.51	1.38	48.1	1.5
17	I feel that my own and others safety is at risk if I make a mistake	2.45	1.17	44.2	2.1
18	The relationship between the contractors and the company men	2.45	1.43	40.8	2.6
19	Feeling trapped into offshore work because no suitable onshore work is available	2.44	1.51	41.3	5.2
20	Boredom — not enough to do	2.40	1.30	42.8	3.6
21	Disturbance in living accommodation due to noise from other people	2.38	1.28	41.5	3.1

Number	Stressor item	Mean score	Standard deviation	% of respondents scoring in 3 – 5 stress range	% of sample responding "non-applicable"
22	Unable to get involved in the community at home (e.g. clubs and organisations)	2.36	1.38	41.5	3.1
23	Working 14 days on/off — day and night shift	2.34	1.26	40.7	34.0
24	Working in a hazardous/dangerous environment	2.33	1.13	39.0	2.1
25	Disruption of my social life	2.33	1.32	38.6	1.0
26	Getting insufficient sleep when I am offshore	2.33	1.27	40.7	2.6
27	Lack of privacy	2.33	1.32	38.6	1.0
28	Sharing living/sleeping accommodation	2.32	1.35	37.7	5.7
29	Sometimes I feel I don't have time to do the job properly	2.32	1.32	37.4	2.1
30	Unpleasant working conditions due to cold	2.29	1.13	39.3	6.7
31	Staying overnight to meet early check-in time	2.27	1.42	35.3	15.5
32	Feeling isolated from home and world events while I am offshore	2.26	1.36	37.6	1.0
33	Working long hours	2.22	1.28	35.1	1.5
34	Frequent changes in my work crew/team	2.2	1.27	39.4	5.7
35	Restricted ability to contact home while I am away	2.18	1.32	35.1	6.2
36	Inadequate instruction to do the job	2.18	1.20	34.3	2.6
37	Inadequate specific training for offshore work	2.17	1.25	36.4	5.2
38	Lack of job satisfaction	2.16	1.21	32.8	2.6
39	Unpleasant working conditions due to heat	2.16	1.17	32.8	7.2
40	I feel it is impossible to make changes concerning my job	2.13	1.19	36.1	5.7
41	Unpleasant working conditions due to vibration	2.12	1.09	36.7	8.8

Number	Stressor item	Mean score	Standard deviation	% of respondents scoring in 3 – 5 stress range	% of sample responding "non-applicable"
42	I don't feel enough is done towards personal safety	2.12	1.15	33.0	3.1
43	The variety and uncertainty in my job	2.11	1.20	33.3	2.6
44	Inadequate facilities for physical exercise	2.11	1.24	32.8	2.6
45	Travel from home to check-in place	2.08	1.32	32.2	1.0
46	Disturbance in living accommodation due to noise from machinery	2.07	1.21	28.7	6.7
47	Problems unwinding when I return home	2.06	1.29	33.2	3.6
48	Disturbance in living accommodation due to heat/cold	2.03	1.15	28.3	3.6
49	Leaving your wife/partner to cope/make decisions	2.0	1.22	28.3	10.8
50	Working in severe weather conditions	2.0	1.10	28.3	5.2
51	The routine nature of my job	1.98	1.01	27.1	1.0
52	Keeping up with changes and new equipment	1.97	1.24	19.8	3.6
53	Travel by helicopter	1.97	1.24	27.4	0
54	The relationship between me and my boss/supervisor	1.97	1.22	26.8	0
55	Long periods of intense concentration	1.94	1.11	25.8	4.1
56	Feeling inadequate when someone has an accident	1.94	1.0	25.8	2.1
57	Feeling restricted/confined	1.91	1.08	24.9	1.0
58	Deterioration in working relationships after intensive periods together	1.91	1.03	23.8	2.6
59	Wife/partner's attitude to me working offshore	1.90	1.22	25.9	8.2
60	Working 7 days on/off — days only	1.89	1.25	27.9	46.4
61	The need to crew change by supply boat	1.86	1.19	26.9	33.0
62	Having to move my wife/family to meet the demands of my job	1.84	1.26	25.2	16.0

Number	Stressor item	Mean score	Standard deviation	% of respondents scoring in 3 – 5 stress range	% of sample responding "non-applicable"
63	Working 7 days on/off — alternate weeks days and nights	1.82	1.11	21.0	68
64	Difficulties concentrating on work when my mind is thinking about home	1.81	1.09	23.4	3.1
65	Disturbance in living accommodation due to vibration	1.80	1.02	19.5	7.7
66	Working 14 days on/off — days	1.80	1.07	27.1	58.2
67	Working relationships within my work crew/team	1.79	1.02	23.9	0.5
68	Having no-one to talk over problems with	1.76	1.08	22.2	4.6
69	Lacking confidence about medical facilities	1.75	1.08	20.0	2.1
70	Difficulties with my children because I work offshore	1.72	1.14	18.5	36.1
71	Having to teach others to do the job	1.7	1.07	15.6	17.0
72	Problems arising because of language/dialect difference	1.7	0.99	14.2	8.8
73	Fear of being branded a trouble maker	1.67	1.03	20.8	5.7
74	Risk of marriage breakdown because I work offshore	1.61	1.06	16.7	25.8
75	Having to discipline people	1.56	0.91	12.7	30.9
76	Working in an all male environment	1.55	0.95	15.1	0.5
77	Women working offshore	1.52	1.09	13.5	31.4
78	Feeling threatened by wife/partner's independence	1.48	0.83	12.5	13.5
79	Mixing and working with people from different countries	1.42	0.75	7.0	8.2
80	Having a working wife	1.35	0.80	8.0	36.1

B. FACTOR ANALYSIS OF THE PSYCHOSOCIAL AND OCCUPATIONAL STRESSOR QUESTIONNAIRE

Factor 1.
Relationships at Work and at Home (24.3% of variance. Eigen value 19.4)

1   Deterioration in working relationships after intensive periods together.
2   The relationship between the "contractor" and the "company" man.
3   Feeling trapped into offshore work because no suitable onshore work is available.
4   Problem unwinding when I return home.
5   Disruption to my social life.
6   Unable to get involved in the community at home (e.g. clubs, organisations).
7   Feeling isolated from home and world events while I am offshore.
8   Difficulties concentrating on work when my mind is thinking about home.

Factor 2.
Site Management Problems (4.8% of variance. Eigen value 3.8)

1   Not getting co-operation at work.
2   Frequent changes in my work crew/team.
3   Problems arising because of language/dialect difference.
4   Having no one to talk over problems with.
5   Inadequate instruction to do the job.
6   Having to discipline people.

Factor 3.
Factors intrinsic to the job (4% of variance. Eigen value 3.2)

1   Working 7 days on/off – alternate weeks of days and nights.
2   Working 14 days on/off – days.
3   Working 28 days on/off.
4   Last minute changes in crew relief arrangements.
5   Staying overnight to meet early check-in time.
6   Unpleasant working conditions due to: – heat.
7   "   "   "   "   " – cold.
8   "   "   "   "   " – vibration.
9   "   "   "   "   " – noise.
10   Disturbance in living accommodation due to: – noise from machinery.
11   "   "   "   "   "   " – vibration.

Factor 4.
The uncertainty element of the work environment (3.6% of variance. Eigen value 2.9)

1   Women working offshore.
2   Working with inadequately trained people.
3   Mixing and working with people from different countries.
4   Rate of pay.
5   Pay differentials.
6   Lack of paid holidays.
7   Inadequate specific training for offshore work.
8   Having to work with people unsuited to offshore life and work.

Factor 5.
Living in the environment (3.0% of variance. Eigen value 2.4)

1   Sharing living/sleeping accommodation.
2   Disturbance in living accommodation due to: – noise from other people.
3   "   "   "   "   "   " – heat/cold.
4   Lack of privacy.

Factor 6.
Safety (2.8% of variance. Eigen value 2.2)

1   Long periods of intense concentration.
2   Keeping up with changes and new equipment.
3   I feel that my own and others safety is at risk if I make a mistake.
4   Travel by helicopter.
5   Lacking confidence about medical facilities.
6   Feeling inadequate when someone has an accident.

Factor 7.
Interface between job and family (2.6% of variance. Eigen value 2.1)

1   Working in an all-male environment.
2   My wife's/partner's attitude to me working offshore.
3   Leaving your wife/partner to cope/make decisions.
4   Feeling threatened by wife/partner's independence.
5   Risk of marriage breakdown because I work offshore.
6   Restricted ability to contact home while I am away.

References

Adams, J. S. (1965) "Inequity in social exchange". In L. Berkowitz (ed.) *Advances in Experimental Social Psychology*, Vol. 2. New York: Academic Press.

Appley, M. H. and Trumbull, R. (1967) *Psychological Stress*. New York: Appleton.

Argyris, C. (1964) *Integrating the Individual and the Organisation*. New York: Wiley.

Arthur, R. J., Gunderson, E. K. (1965) "Promotion and Mental Illness in the Navy". *Journal of Occupational Medicine*, 7, 452–456.

Attfield, K. "How Safe are North Sea Platforms?" *New Scientist*, 64, October, 1974, 192–196.

Bamber, L. (1981) "Risk Management and Loss Control" in S. S. Chissick and R. Derricott (eds.) *Occupational Health and Safety Management*. U.K.: John Wiley.

Beehr, T. A. and Newman, J. E. (1978) "Job Stress, Employee Health and Organisational Effectiveness: A facet analysis model and literature review", *Personnel Psychology*, 31, 665–699.

Berman, A. M. (1981) "Safety — so far as is reasonably practicable", in S. S. Chissick and R. Derricott (eds.) *Occupational Health and Safety Management*. U.K.: Wiley.

Bernard, C. (1865) *An introduction to the Study of Experimental Medicine*, translated by H. C. Greene. London: Macmillan, 1927.

Bernard, J. (1968) "The Eudaenomists". In S. Z. Klausner (ed.) *Why Man Takes Chances*, Garden City, New York: Anchor (Doubleday).

Bhagat, R. S. (1983) "Effects of Stressful Life Events upon Individual Performance Effectiveness and Work Adjustment Processes within Organisational Settings: A Research Model". *Academy of Management Review*, 8, (4), 660–671.

Bohemier (1985) "Mar-Tech, 1985 Montreal". Reported *Lloyd's List*, May 23rd, 1985.

- Boucheny, L. (1983) "The risk of accident in the oil and gas extractive industries". In the International Symposium Proceedings, *Safety & Health in the Oil & Gas Extractive Industries*, Luxembourg, April 1983. London: Graham and Trotman.

Brebner, J. and Cooper, C. (1979) "Stimulus or response induced excitation: A comparison of behaviour of introverts and extraverts". *Journal of Research into Personality*, 12, 306–11.

Brief, A. P., Schuler, R. S. and Van Self, M. (1981) *Managing Job Stress*. Boston: Little, Brown & Co.

Breslow, L. and Buell, P. (1960) "Mortality from Coronary Heart Disease and Physical Activity of Work in California". *Journal of Chronic Diseases*, 11, 615–26.

Brook, A. (1973) "Mental Stress at Work". *The Practitioner*, 210, 500–506.

Buck, V. (1972) *Working Under Pressure*. London: Staples Press.

Burke, R. G. "The unseen side of safety training". *Offshore*, August 1985.

Bustin, H. E. (1983) "Environmental Health Requirements on Offshore Oil & Gas Exploration & Production Installations". International Symposium, Luxembourg. *Op. cit.*

Cannon, W. B. (1932) *The Wisdom of the Body*. New York: W.W. Norton.

Cannon, W. B. (1935) "Stresses and strain of homeostasis". *American Journal of Medical Science*, 189, (1).

Caplan, G. (1964) *Principles of Preventive Psychiatry*. London: Tavistock.

Caplan, R. (1971) *Organisational Stress and Individual Strain: A social-psychosocial study of risk factors in coronary disease among administrators, engineers and scientists*. Ann Arbor, Michigan Research Centre For Group Dynamics.

Caplan, R. D. (1983) "Person-Environment Fit: Past, present and future". In C. L. Cooper (ed.) *Stress Research, Issues for the Eighties*. Chichester and New York: Wiley.

Caplan, R. D., Cobb, S., French, J. R. P., Van Harrison, R. and Pinneau, S. R. "Job Demands and Worker Health: Main Effects and Occupational Differences". *NIOSH Research Report*, 1975.

Carruthers, M. (1980) "Hazardous Occupations and the Heart". In C.L. Cooper and R. Payne (eds.) *Current Concerns in Occupational Stress*. U.K.: John Wiley.

Cassel, J. C. (1970) "The contribution of the social environment to host resistance". *American Journal of Epidemiology*, 104, 107–123.

Chan, K. B. (1977) "Individual Differences in Reactions to Stress and their Personality and Situational Detriments". *Social Science and Medicine*, 11, 89–103.

Cherry, N. (1978) "Stress, Anxiety and Work: Longitudinal Study". *Journal of Occupational Psychology*, 51, 259–270.

Chesney, M. A. and Rosenman, R. H. (1980) "Type A Behaviour in the Work Setting". In C. L. Cooper and R. Payne (eds.) *Current Concerns in Occupational Stress*. U.K.: John Wiley.

Child, D. (1976) *The Essentials of Factor Analysis*. New York: Holt, Rinehart and Winston.

Chissick, S. S. and Derricott, R. (eds.) *Occupational Health and Safety Management*. UK: John Wiley, 1981.

Cofer, C. N. and Appley, M. H. (1964) *Motivation, Theory and Research*. New York: Wiley.

Cooper, C. L. (1973) *Group Training for Individual and Organisational Development*. Switzerland: S. Karger.

Cooper, C. L. (1978) "Dentists Under Pressure: A Social Psychological Study". *Journal of Occupational Psychology*, 51, (3), 227–234.

Cooper C. L. (1981) *The Stress Check*. U.S.A.: Prentice Hall.

Cooper, C. L. (1981) *Executive Families Under Stress*. U.S.A.: Prentice Hall.

Cooper, C. L. (ed.) *Stress Research Issues for the Eighties*. U.K.: John Wiley (1983).

Cooper, C. L. (1983) "Identifying stressors at work: Recent research developments". *Journal of Psychosomatic Research*, 17, (5), 369–376.

Cooper, C. L. (1984) "What's New In Stress". *Personnel Management*, June 1984.

Cooper, C. L. (1985) "The Stress of Work: An overview". *Aviation, Space and Environmental Medicine*, July, 627–632.

Cooper, C. L. and Marshall, J. (1978) *Understanding Executive Stress*. U.K.: Macmillan.

Cooper, J. C. B. (1984) "The Oil Industry in Scotland". *Scottish Bankers' Magazine*, November 1984.

Corson, S. A. (1971) "The lack of feedback in today's societies — a psychosocial stressor". In L. Levi (ed.) *Society, stress and disease*, Vol. 1. London: Oxford University Press.

Cox, V. C., Paulus, P. B., McCain, G., Karlovac, M. "The Relationship between Crowding and Health". In A. Baum and J. Singer (eds.) *Advances in Experimental Psychology*, Vol. 4. U.S.A.: Lawrence Earlbaum, 1982.

Cox, W. M. (2979) "The alcohol personality: A review of the evidence". *Progress in Experimental Personality Research*, 9, 89–148.

Crisp, A. H. and Priest, R. G. (1971) "Psycho-neurotic Profiles in Middle Age". *British Journal of Psychiatry*, 199, 385–392.

Crisp, A. H. (1977) "Psycho-neurotics in the General Population". *Journal International Medical Research*, 5, Supplement (4), 61–80.

Crisp, A. H., Gaynor-Jones, M. and Slater, P. (1978a) "The Middlesex Hospital Questionnaire: A validity study". *British Journal of Medical Psychology*, 51, 269–280.

Crown, S. and Crisp, A. H. (1966) "A short clinical diagnostic self rating scale for psychoneurotic patients". *British Journal of Psychiatry*, 112, 917–923.

Crown, S., Duncan, K. P., Howell, R. W. (1970) "Further Evaluation of the Middlesex Hospital Questionnaire (MHQ)". *British Journal of Psychiatry*, 116, 33–7.

Crown, S. (1974) "The Middlesex Hospital Questionnaire in clinical research: A review". In Pichot, P. (ed.) *Psychological Measurements in Psychopharmacology*. Basel: S. Karger, 111–124.

Crown, S., Crisp, A. H. (1979) *Manual of the Crown-Crisp Experiential Index*. London: Hodder and Stoughton.

Crump, J. H., Cooper, C. L. and Smith, M. (1980) "Investigating occupational stress: A methodological approach". *Journal of Occupational Behaviour*, 1 (3) 191–204.

Davidson, M. J., Veno, A. (1980) "Stress and the Policeman" in C.L. Cooper and J. Marshall (eds.) *White Collar and Professional Stress*. London: John Wiley.

Diebold, J. (1964) *Beyond Automation*. New York: McGraw Hill.

Dohrenwend, B. S. and Dohrenwend, B. P. (1974) *Stressful Life Events*. New York: Wiley.

Donovan, D. M. and O'Leary, M. R. (1983) "Control Orientation, Drinking Behaviour and Alcoholism". In H. M. Lefcourt (ed.) *Research with the Locus of Control Construct* (Vol. 2), *Development and Social Problems*. U.K.: Academic Press.

Dunbar, F. (1943) *Psychosomatic Medicine*. New York: Hoeber.

Elliott, D. H. (1985) "The Offshore Worker". *The Practitioner*, 229, June, 565–571.

Erikson, J., Pugh, W. M., Gunderson, E. K. "Status Congruency as a Predictor of Job Satisfaction and Life Stress". *Journal of Applied Psychology*, 56, 523–525.

Evans, G. W. (1979) "Behavioural and Physiological Consequences of Crowding in Humans". *Journal of Applied Social Psychology*, 9, (1), 27–46.

Eysenck, H. J. (1947) *Dimensions of Personality*. London: Routledge and Kegan Paul.

Fentem, P. H. and Bassey, E. J. *The Case for Exercise*. Sports Council Research Working Papers, No. 8, London, 1979.

Fine, B. J. (1963) "Introversion, extraversion and motor driver behaviour". *Perceptual and Motor Skills*, 16, 95.

Flamholtz, E. "Should your organisation attempt to value its human resources?". *California Review*, 1971.

Forum, E. and P., Patterson, G. R. (1983) "Safety and Health Offshore: A survey of North Sea Legislation". International Symposium, Luxembourg. *Op. cit.*

Frankenhaeuser, M. (1976) *Quality of Life: Criteria for Behavioural Adjustment*. Report from the Department of Psychology, University of Stockholm (No. 475).

French, J. R. P. (1973) "Person-Role-Fit", *Occupational Mental Health*, 3, 1.

French, J. R. P., and Caplan, R. D. (1970) "Psychosocial Factors in Coronary Heart Disease". *Industrial Medicine*, 39, 383–397.

French, J. R. P., and Caplan, R. D. (1973) "Organisational Stress and Individual Strain". In Marrow (ed.) *The Failure of Success*. New York: Amacon, pp 30–66.

Frère, J. J. (1975) "Conditions of Work on Board North Sea Oil Prospection Vessels". Faculté de Medecine, Lille, France. MD Thesis.

Friedman, M. (1969) *Pathogenesis of Coronary Artery Disease*. New York: McGraw Hill.

Friedman, M. and Rosenman, R. H. (1974) *Type A: Your Behaviour and Your Heart*. New York: Knopf.

Gentile, G., Cazzola, Schenato, A., Torricelli (1983) *An overview of safety training for onshore and offshore working*. Proceedings International Symposium, Luxembourg, April, 1983.

Gillespie, F. (1974) "Stress Costs More than Strikes". *Financial Times*, April 26, 1974.

Glass, D. C. and Singer, J. E. (1972) *Urban Stress: Experiments on Noise and Social Stressors*. New York: Academic Press.

Glowinkowski, S. P., and Cooper, C. L. "Current issues in organisational stress research". *Bulletin of the British Psychological Society* (1985), 38, 212–216.

Gogstad, Hellesøy, Odd, H., Eide (1981) "Marital Status — Statfjord A" in *Work Environment Statfjord Field*. Universitetsforlaget, Bergen, 1985.

Graeven, D. B. (1975) "Necessity control and predictability of noise annoyance". *Journal of Social Psychology*, 95, 85–90.

Gregg, M. G. (1985) "An investigation of the locus of control construct: Theoretical Developments and their application to work". Ph.D Thesis. University of Manchester.

Griest, H. H., Klein, M. H., Eischens, R. R., Faris, J. W. (1978) "Antidepressant Running", *Behavioural Medicine*, 5 (6), 19–24.

Gunderson, E. K., Eric (1978) "Organisational Environmental Influences on Health and Performance" in B. T. King, S. Strenfert and F. E. Fielder (eds.) *Managerial Control and Organisational Democracy*. New York: Halstead Press, pp. 43–60.

Hackman, J. R. and Oldham, G. R. (1975) "Development of the job diagnostic survey". *Journal of Applied Psychology*, 60, 159–170.

Hall, D. T. (1976) *Careers in Organisations*. U.S.A.: Goodyear.

Hall, D. T., and Hall, F. S. (1980) "Stress and the Two-Career Couple" in C. L. Cooper and R. Payne (eds.) *Current Concerns in Occupational Stress*. New York: Wiley, pp. 243–266.

Hammond, E. C. (1964) "Some preliminary findings on physical complaints from a prospective study of 1,064,004 men and women". *American Journal of Public Health*, 54, 1.

Handy, C. (1978) "The Family: Help or Hindrance" in C. L. Cooper and R. Payne (eds.) *Stress at Work*. New York: Wiley, 107–123.

Harrison, R. V., (1975) "Job stress and worker health: person-environment misfit". Paper presented to the American Public Health Association Convention. Chicago.

Haynes, S. G., Levine, S., Scotch, N., Feinleib, M. and Kannel, W. B. (1978a) "The relationship of psychosocial factors to coronary heart disease in the Framingham Study 1. Methods and risk Factors." *American Journal of Epidemiology*, 197, 362–383.

Haynes, S. G., Feinleib, M., Levine, S., Scotch, N., and Kennel, W. B. (1978b) "The relationship of psychosocial factors to coronary heart disease in the Framingham Study II. Prevalence of coronary heart disease". *American Journal of Epidemiology*, 107, 384–402.

Haynes, S. G., Feinleib, M. and Kannel, W. B. (1980) "The relationship of psychosocial factors to coronary heart disease in the Framingham Study III. Eight-year incidence of coronary heart disease". *American Journal of Epidemiology*, 111, 37–58.

Hellesøy, Odd, H. (1985) *Work Environment Statfjord Field*. Universitetsforlaget, Bergen.

Hellesøy, Odd, H. (1985) "Stress of the Offshore Worker". Paper presented at the International Rig Medic Conference, Aberdeen, June 1985.

Hennigan, J. K. and Wortham, A. W. (1975) "Analysis of workday stress on industrial managers using heart rate as a criteria". *Ergonomics*, 18, 675–681.

Herzberg, F. (1978) "The Human Need for Work". *Industry Week*, July 24, 49–52.

Hinkle, L. E. (1973) "The Concept of 'Stress' in the Biological and Social Sciences". *Science, Medicine and Man*, 1, 31–48.

Hirschfeld, A. H. and Behan, R. C. (1963) "The Accident Process: Etiological Considerations of Industrial Injuries". *Journal of the American Medical Association*, 186, 193–199.

Hirschfeld, A. H. and Behan, R. C. (1966) "The Accident Process III. Disability: Acceptable and Unacceptable". *Journal of the American Medical Association*, 197, 125–129.

H.M.S.O. (1985) *Development of the Oil and Gas Resources of the United Kingdom, 1985*.

House, J. S. (1972) "The Relationship of Intrinsic and Extrinsic Work Motivation to Occupational Stress and Coronary Heart Disease Risk". Ph.D Dissertation, University of Michigan.

House, J. S. (1974b) "Occupational stress and coronary heart disease: a review and theoretical integration". *Journal of Health and Social Behaviour,* 5, 12–27.

House, J. S. (1981) *Work Stress and Social Support.* U.S.A.: Addison-Wesley.

Howard, J. H., Cunningham, D. A. and Rechnitzer, P. A. (1976) "Health patterns associated with Type 'A' behaviour; A managerial population". *Journal of Human Stress,* 2, 24–31.

Hoyland, A. (1976) Institute of Marine Engineers Conference on Noise and Vibration, October 21, 1976.

Hurrell, J. J. and Kroes, W. H. (1975) *Stress Awareness.* Cincinnati, Ohio: National Institute for Occupational Safety and Health.

Immundo, L. V. (1974) "Problems Associated with Managerial Mobility". *Personnel Journal,* 53, (12) 910.

Innes, J. M. (1981) "Social Psychological Approaches to the Study of the Induction and Alleviation of Stress: Influences upon Health and Illness" in G. M. Stephenson and J. M. Davies (eds.) *Progress in Applied Social Psychology.* Vol. 1. U.K.: John Wiley.

International Labour Office (1978) *Safety Problems in the Offshore Petroleum Industry.* Geneva: ILO.

International Labour Office (1983) *Accident Prevention. A workers education manual.* Geneva: ILO.

Ivancevich, J. M. and Matteson, M. T. (1980) *Stress at Work.* U.S.A.: Scott, Foresman.

Janis, I. L. and Mann, L. (1965) "Effectiveness of emotional role playing in modifying smoking habits and attitudes". *Journal of Experimental Research in Personality,* 1, 84–90.

Jenkins, C. D. (1971a) "Psychologic and Social Precursors of Coronary Disease". *New England Journal of Medicine,* 284, (5), 244–255.

Jenkins, C. D. (1971b) "Psychologic Social Precursors of Coronary Disease". *New England Journal of Medicine,* 284 (6), 307–317.

Jenkins, C. D. (1976) "Recent evidence supporting psychologic and social risk factors for coronary disease". *New England Journal of Medicine,* 294, 1033–1036.

Joe, V. C. (1971) "Review of the internal-external control constructs as a personality variable". *Psychological Reports,* 28, 619–640.

Jones, C. (1983) "An Overview of health aspects of the onshore and offshore oil and gas extractive industries". International Symposium, Luxembourg.

Jones, D. M. (1983) "Noise" in R. Hockey (ed.) *Stress and Fatigue in Human Performance.* U.K.: John Wiley.

Kabanoff, B. (1980) "Work and non-work: A review of models, methods and findings". *Psychological Bulletin,* 88 (1), 60–77.

Kahn, R. L., Wolfe, D. M., Quinn, R. P., Snoek, J. D., Rosenthal, R. A. (1964) *Organisational Stress: Studies in Role Conflict and Ambiguity.* U.K.: John Wiley, p. 41.

Karasek, R. A. Jr. (1979) "Job Demands, Job Decision Latitude and Mental Strain: Implications for Job re-design". *Administrative Science Quarterly,* Vol. 24, 285–308.

Kasl, S. V., Cobb, S. (1970) "Blood Pressure Changes in Men Undergoing Job Loss: A Preliminary Report". *Psychosomatic Medicine,* 32, 19–38.

Kasl, S. V. (1973) "Mental Health and Work Environment. An examination of the evidence". *Journal of Occupational Medicine*, 15, 506–515.

Kasl, S. V. (1978) "Epidemiological Contributions to the Study of Work Stress" in C. L. Cooper and R. Payne (eds.) *Stress at Work*. U.K.: John Wiley.

Kelly, M., Cooper, C. L. (1981) "Stress among Blue Collar Workers. A case study of the steel industry". *Employee Relations*, 3, (2), 6–9.

Kerlinger, F. N. (1970) *Foundations of Behavioural Research*. New York: Holt, Rinehart and Winston.

Kerlinger, F. N. and Pedhazer, E. (1973) *Multiple Regression in Behavioural Research*. New York: Holt, Rinehart and Winston.

Kornhauser, A. (1965) *Mental Health of the Industrial Worker*. New York: Wiley.

Krantz, D. S. (1978) *Coronary artery disease and coronary prone behaviour*. Progress Report to the National Heart, Lung and Blood Institute.

Kreitman, N. (1968) "Married Couples Admitted to Mental Hospital". *British Journal of Psychiatry*, 114, 699–718.

Kummer, R. (1983) "Noise in oil and gas extractive industries". International Symposium, Luxembourg. *Op. cit.*

Lazarus, R. S. (1966) *Psychological Stress and the Coping Process*. New York: McGraw Hill.

Lazarus, R. S. (1971) "The Concepts of Stress and Disease" in L. Levi (ed.) *Society, Stress and Disease*, Vol. 1. London: Oxford University Press, pp. 53–60.

Lefcourt, H. M. (1976) *Locus of Control*. U.K.: Wiley.

Lefcourt, H. M. (1982) *Locus of Control. Current Trends in Theory and Research*, 2nd Edition, London. New Jersey: Lawrence Erlbaum.

Lefcourt, H. M. (1983) *Research and the locus of control construct*. Vol. 2, *Developments and Social Problems*. U.K.: Academic Press.

Levi, L. (1967) *Stress: Sources, management and prevention; medical and psychological aspects of the stress of everyday life*. New York: Liveright.

Levinson, D. J. (1978) *The Seasons of a Man's Life*. U.S.A.: Alfred A. Knopf.

Levinson, H. (1978) "The Abrasive Personality". *The Harvard Business Review*, 56, May-June, 86–94.

Lewin, K., Lippitt, R. and White, R. K. (1939) "Patterns of Aggressive Behaviour in Experimentally Created Social Climates". *Journal of Social Psychology*, 10, 271–299.

Livy, B. and Vant, J. "Formula for selecting roughnecks and roustabouts". *Personnel Management*, February, 1979.

Lynch, S., Folkins, C. H. and Wilmore, J. H. (1975) "Relationships between three mood variables and physical exercise". Unpublished data, February, 1973.

Mackay, G. M., De Foneka, C. P., Blair, I. and Clayton, A. B. (1969) *Causes and Effects of Road Accidents*. Department of Transportation, University of Birmingham.

Margolis, B., Kroes, W. and Quinn, R. (1974) "Job stress an unlisted occupational hazard". *Journal of Occupational Medicine*, 1, (16), 659–661.

Matheson, D. W., Bruce, R. L., Beauchamp, K. L. (1978) *Experimental Psychology. Research Design and Analysis*, 3rd Edition. U.S.A.: Holt, Rinehart and Winston.

McClelland, D. C. N. (1965) "Achievement and entrepeneurship: A longitudinal stud /". *Journal of Personality and Social Psychology*, 1, 389–392.

McCrae, R. R., Costa, P. T. and Bosse, R. (1978) "Anxiety, extraversion and smoking". *British Journal of Social and Clinical Psychology*, 17, 269–273.

McGrath, J. E. (1970) "A Conceptual Formulation for Research on Stress" in J. E. McGrath (ed.) *Social and Psychological Factors on Stress*. New York: Holt, Rinehart and Winston, pp. 10–21.

McGrath, J. E. "Stress and behaviour in organisations" in M. D. Dunnette (ed.), *Handbook of Industrial and Organisational Psychology*. Chicago: Rand McNally, 1976.

McLean, A. A. (1979) *Work Stress*. U.S.A. Addison-Wesley.

McMichael, A. J. (1978) "Personality, Behavioural and Situational Modifiers of Work Stressors" in C. L. Cooper and R. Payne (eds.) *Stress at Work*. U.K.: John Wiley.

Mischel, W. (1976) *Introduction to Personality*, 2nd Edition. New York: Holt, Rinehart, Winston.

Monk, T. H. and Folkard, S. (1983) "Circadian Rhythms and Shiftwork" in Robert Hockey (ed.) *Stress and Fatigue in Human Performance*. U.K.: John Wiley.

Moore, R. and Wybrow, R. (1984) *Women in the North Sea Oil Industry*. U.K.: Equal Opportunities Commission.

Mueller, E. F. (1965) *Psychological and physiological correlates of work overload among university professors, umpublished doctoral dissertation*. University of Michigan, Ann Arbor.

Neff, W. S. (1968) *Work and Human Behaviour*. New York: Atherton Press.

Nie, N. H., Hull, C. H., Jenkins, J. G., Steinbrenner, K., Bent, D. H. (1975) *SPSS — Statistical Package for the Social Sciences*, 2nd Edition, U.S.A. London: McGraw-Hill.

Nisbet, R. A. (1962) *Community and Power*. London: Oxford University Press, p. 73.

Norman, J., Nelson, Brebner, J. (1985) *The Offshore Health Handbook*. U.K.: Martin Dunitz, pp. 16–17.

Noroil, January, 1985 "Offshore systems for safety". Norway: *Noroil*, 57–60.

Oborne, D. J. (1982) *Ergonomics at Work*. U.K.: John Wiley.

Office of Health Economics: *Compendium of health statistics*, 3rd Edition, 1979. London: H.M.S.O.

Offshore Oil and Gas Yearbook, 1983/84: U.K. and Continental Europe. U.K.: Benn Technical Books, 1983.

Ojeslo, L. (1980) "The Relationship to Alcoholism of Occupational Class and Employment" in *Journal of Occupational Medicine*, 22, (10), 657–666.

Opbrock, H. A. (1983) "Men and Materials Handling in Offshore Operations". International Symposium, Luxembourg. *Op. cit.*

Osler, W. (1910) "Angina pectoris". *Lancet*, i, 839.

Otten, M. W. (1977) "Inventory and expressive measure of locus of control and academic performance". *Journal of Personality Assessment*, 41, 644–649.

Owens, D. A. (1969) Disability — minority and social learning. Unpublished Master's thesis, West Virginia University.

Packard, V. (1972) *A Nation of Strangers*. New York: McKay.

Pahl, J. M. and Pahl, R. E. (1971) *Managers and their Wives*. London: Allen Lane.

Philbert, M., Frére, J. J. and Emmanueli, X. (1975) "Working, Living and Medical Conditions Aboard an Oil Barge in the North Sea". *Archives de maladies progressionnelles de medecine du travail et de Securite* (Paris), 36, (3), 137–144,

Pincherle, G. (1972) "Fitness for Work". *Proceedings of the Royal Society of Medicine*, 65, (4), 321–324.

Plant, M. A. (1979) "Occupations, Drinking Patterns and Alcohol-Related Problems: Conclusions from a follow up study". *British Journal of Addiction*, 74, (3), 267–273.

Poulton, E. C. (1978) "Blue Collar Stressors" in C. L. Cooper and R. Payne (eds.) *Stress at Work*. U.K.: John Wiley.

Proceedings of an International Symposium on Safety and Health in the Oil and Gas Extractive Industries, Luxembourg, April, 1983: published by Graham and Trotman: London.

Prossin, A. (1983) "The Ocean and Occupational Health". *Canadian Family Physician*, Vol. 29, 1135–1140.

Quick, J. C., and Quick J. D. (1984) *Organisational Stress and Preventive Management*. U.S.A.: McGraw-Hill.

Ramsey, J. D. (1983) "Heat and Cold" in Robert Hockey (ed.) *Stress and Fatigue in Human Performance*. U.K.: Wiley.

Reddin, J. (1985) "Safety at Sea". *Offshore International Journal of Ocean Business*, August, 43–51.

Roethlisberger, F. and Dickson, J. J. (1939) "Management and the Worker". Cambridge, Mass.: Harvard University Press.

Rosenmann, R. H., Friedman, M. and Strauss, R. (1964) "A predictive study of C.H.D.". *Journal of the American Medical Association*, 189, 15–22.

Rosenmann, R. H., Friedman, M. and Strauss, R. (1966) "C.H.D. in the Western Collaborative Group Study". *Journal of the American Medical Association*, 195, 86–92.

Rosenmann, R. H., Brand, R. H., Jenkins, D., Friedman, M., Strauss, R., and Wurm, M. (1975) "Coronary heart disease in the Western Collaborative Group Study. Final follow up experience of 8.5 years". *Journal of the Amercian Medical Association*, 233, 875–877.

Ross, B. C. (1978) "Noise on offshore platforms". *Occupational Health*, 30, (11), 524–527.

Rotter, J. B. (1966) "Generalised expectancies for internal versus external control of reinforcement". *Psychological Monographs*, 80, (1), whole no. 609.

Roythorne, C. (1983) "Routine Examination of Offshore Workers". International Symposium, Luxembourg. *Op. cit.*

Russeck, H. I. and Zohman, B. L. (1958) "Relative significance of heredity, diet and occupational stress in C.H.D. of young adults". *Amercian Journal of Medical Sciences*, 235, 266–275.

Salancik, G. R. and Pfeffer, J. A. (1978) "A social information processing approach to job attitude and task design". *Administrative Science Quarterly*, 23, 224–253.

Sales, S. M. (1969) "Differences among Individuals in Affective Behavioural, Biochemical and Physiological Responses to Variations in Work Load". Ph.D. Thesis, University of Michigan.

Sales, S. M (1970) "Some effects of role overload and role underload". *Organisational Behaviour and Human Performance*, 5, 592–608.

Sartre, J. P. (1947). *Huis Clos*. Paris: Theatre Gallimard.

Schmidt, R. T. (1976) "Safe Employees are well adjusted people". *Occupational Health and Safety*, June 1976, p. 38.

Schuler, R. S. (1980) "Definition and Conceptualisation of Stress in Organisations". *Organisational Behaviour and Human Performance*, 25, 184–215.

Seashore, S. E. (1954) *Group Cohesiveness in the Industrial Work Group*. Ann Arbor: Institute for Social Research, University of Michigan.

Seashore, S. E. (1972) "A survey of working conditions in the United States". *Studies in Personnel Psychology*, 4, 7–19.

Selye, H. (1956) *The Stress of Life*. U.S.A.: McGraw-Hill.

Selye, H. (1973) "The evolution of the stress concept". *American Scientist*, 61, 692–699.

Selye, H. (1974) *Stress without Distress*. Philadelphia: J. B. Lippincott.

Selye, H. (1976) *Stress in Health and Disease*. London: Butterworths.

Selye, H. (1976b) *Stress in Health and Disease*. Boston: Butterworths.

Selye, H. (1983) "The Stress Concept: Past, Present and Future", in C. L. Cooper (ed.) *Stress Research*. U.K.: John Wiley (1983).

Shirom, A., Eden, D., Silberwasser, S. and Kellerman, J. J. (1973) "Job Stress and Risk Factors in Coronary Heart Disease Among Occupational Categories in Kibbutzim". *Social Science and Medicine*, 7, 875–892.

Sims, M. T., Graves, R. J. and Simpson, G. C. (1984) "Mineworkers scores for the Rotter Internal-External Locus of Control Scale". *Journal of Occupational Psychology*, 57, 327–329.

Sunde, A. (1983) "Psychosocial aspects of offshore work". International Symposium, Luxembourg. *Op. cit.*

Sundstrom, E. (1977) "Interpersonal Behaviour and the physical environment" in L. Wrightsman (ed.) *Social Psychology*. U.S.A.: Brooks Cole.

Taylor, R. (1974) "Stress at Work". *New Society*, October 17, 1974.

Theorell, T. (1976) "Selected illness and somatic factors in relation to two psychosocial stress indices — a prospective study on middle aged construction building workers". *Journal of Psychosomatic Research*, 20, 7–20.

Tinning, R. J., and Spry, W. B. (1981) "The Extent and Significance of Stress Symptoms in Industry — with examples from the Steel Industry" in E. N. Corlett and J. Richardson (eds.) *Stress, Work Design and Productivity*. U.K.: John Wiley.

Toffler, A. (1970) *Future Shock*. U.K.: Pan.

Toffler, A. (1980) *The Third Wave*. U.K.: Pan

Van Harrison, R. (1975) "Job Stress and Worker Health: Person Environment Misfit". Paper presented at the 103rd Annual Meeting of the American Public Health Association. Chicago.

Van Sell, M., Brief, A. P. and Schuler, R. S. (1981) "Role Conflict and Role Ambiguity: 'Integration of the Literature and Directions for Future Research'." *Human Relations*, 34, (1), 43–71.

Verhaegen, P., Vanhalst, B., Derycke, H., and Van Hoecke, M. (1976) "The value of some psychological theories of industrial acidents". *Journal of Occupational Psychology*, 1, 39–45.

Volicer, B. J. (1974) "Patients' perceptions of stressful events associated with hospitalisation". *Nursing Research*, 23, 235–238.

Wardwell, W. J., Hyman, M. and Bahnson, C. B. (1964) "Stress and Coronary Disease in Three Field Studies". *Journal of Chronic Diseases*, 17, 73–84.

Warr, P., Cook, J. and Wall, T. (1979) "Scales for the measurement of some work attitudes and aspects of psychological wellbeing". *Journal of Occupational Psychology*, 52, 129–148.

Warshaw, L. J. (1979) *Managing Stress*. Reading, Mass.: Addison Wesley.

Whitlock, F. A., Stoll, J. R. and Rekhdahl, R. J. (1977) "Crisis of Life Events and Accidents". *Australian and New Zealand Journal of Psychiatry*, Vol. 11, p. 127.

Womack, R. (1985) "An appreciative investment". *Scottish Business Insider*, Vol. 2, No. 3, March 1985.

World Health Organisation Statistics — Quarterly Report, Vol. 35, No. 1, 1982.

Yerkes, R. M. and Dodson, J. D. (1908) "The relation to the strength of the stimulus to the rapidity of habit formation". *Journal of Comparative Neurology and Psychology*, 18, 459–482.

Young, J. P. R., Fenton, G. W. and Lader, M. H. (1971) "The inheritance of neurotic traits. A twin study of the Middlesex Hospital Questionnaire". *British Journal of Psychiatry*, 119, 393–398.

Yvarote, P. M., McDonheh, T. J., Goldman, M. J. and Zuckerman, M. (1974) "Organisation and Evaluation of a Fitness Programme in Industry". *Journal of Occupational Medicine*, 16, (9), 589–598.

Zaleznik, A., Kets de Vries, M. F. R. and Howard, J. (1977) "Stress Reactions in Organisations: Syndromes, causes and consequences". *Behavioural Science*, 22, 151–161.

Zuckerman, M. (1974) "The Sensation Seeking Motive" in *Progress in Experimental Personality Research*, Vol. 7. New York: Academic Press, pages 80–148.

Index